WONDER SEEKER

WONDER SEEKER

52 Ways to Wake Up Your Creativity
+ find your joy

ANDREA SCHER

FOREWORD BY SARK

HARPER
DESIGN

An Imprint of HarperCollins Publishers

WONDER SEEKER

HarperCollins books may be purchased for educational, business, or sales promotional use. For information, please email the Special Markets Department at SPsales@harpercollins.com.

First published in 2021 by
Harper Design
An Imprint of HarperCollins*Publishers*
195 Broadway
New York, NY 10007
Tel: (212) 207-7000
Fax: (855) 746-6023
harperdesign@harpercollins.com
www.hc.com

Distributed throughout the world by
HarperCollins*Publishers*
195 Broadway
New York, NY 10007

ISBN 978-0-06-307382-1

Library of Congress Control Number: 2021010919

Book design by Stislow Design

Printed in Malaysia

First Printing, 2021

PHOTOGRAPHY CREDITS
page 76: Photograph by Jess Weems Thibault
page 140: Photograph by Eve Hannah
page 159: Photograph by Michael Hrostoski
page 176: Photograph by John Nieto
page 203: Photograph by Brigette Scheel
page 208 and back cover: Author photograph by In Her Image Photography
All other photographs by Andrea Scher

THIS BOOK IS DEDICATED TO

Ben and Nico,

MORE WONDROUS THAN
A MILLION SHOOTING STARS.

Contents

I first met Andrea, the ultimate Wonder Seeker and finder (and the author of this book), in the nineties when she applied for a job at my creative company, then called Camp SARK. She shares the absolute wonder of that story in this book!

Knowing and loving Andrea has exponentially expanded my feelings of wonder in this world. I'm so excited for you that her book has burst into your world to do the same.

IT'S A BEACON OF JOY IN A BOOK.

If you have ever wondered how to have more joy and adventure in your life, this book is your portable magic maker, and it's also like going on super fun adventures with Andrea. You will discover new things, attune to color, and experience the world as magical—which includes the real practical things too.

Andrea is a gifted storyteller and healer and is generous with her stories—she gets vulnerable on your behalf and is willing to share some of the hard stuff so that you remember and know that you are not alone.

This book will show you pathways to joy that are both fun and easy—but this isn't about looking only on the bright side or avoiding pain. Andrea is wise enough to know that we have the capacity to be with ALL of it, and shares how to continually seek wonder as part of that all. And all of the best things that we begin or do spring from that sense of wonder.

Andrea is one of those rare souls who see with love eyes and go into the dark and illuminate it.

Her spirit is fresh and bright, and she's that friend you knew—or wish you knew—when you were ten and found fairy paths in the forest near your house, and then wrote them tiny letters that you tucked into the moss near their homes. Now she's a powerfully evolved grown-up friend who consistently seeks and finds wonders and shows you how to do the same in your life.

This book will develop your WONDER EYES and show you how to see and experience so many wonders in your ordinary days too, and you'll be sharing these gifts with all of the souls in your life.

Andrea is a deep and dear soul, and I am honored to call her my friend, and to have created this foreword for her book. Witnessing her life as an artist, writer, photographer, and mom is such a pure blessing; she just radiates love, and so does this book.

Welcome in to these inspiring, depthful, and sparkling-with-possibilities-for-you pages.

What was your first experience of wonder?

For some, it's the first time they saw the night sky on a camping trip. Or that time there were hundreds of tiny sand dollars strewn across the wet sand at the beach. For a friend, it was when her elementary school bus driver stopped the bus at the side of the road so they could all watch a cow giving birth in a field. For another, it was when her father built a kiln in a firepit at their campsite so they could make pottery.

We tend to lose this sense of wonder as we grow older. Perhaps it's cynicism and stress that cloud our view. Maybe we are too busy and think that wonder is only for children. Maybe we think we've seen it all and nothing could surprise us anymore. But here's what I know: *our capacity for wonder and delight is also the gateway to our joy.*

It is vital to our aliveness. It is worth cultivating and honing because our lives become so much richer for it. It is a kind of love and attention. It is a reverence for our world. It's a celebration of being here and a desire to protect this place we call home.

I want you to remember your curiosity and your wide-eyed delight. I want you to know that you are a creative creature who can experience the magic of the everyday world. On one level, it's a shift in attention. And a practice (just like seated meditation) where we continue to pull our focus back from the distractions, the noise, the chaotic swirl of our thoughts—back to the moment. To what is here. What there is to appreciate. What there is to delight in.

For me, Wonder Seeking has been an antidote to an anxious and sensitive system. I am a *very* anxious creature. It took me a while to figure this out— the shortness of breath, the ambient worry—I didn't recognize it as anxiety at first but as a flaw in my character. Something that made me impossible to be with at times—overly sensitive, agitated, unable to settle in my own skin.

tiny sand dollar!

I tried managing my anxiety with walking and yoga. These activities staved off panic and offered some relief, but it was creative practices that always helped the most. I could feel anxious for days, not able to take a full breath, but if I sat down and painted or walked around taking photos, the anxiety would lift almost immediately. Much of my creative life was born out of this need for art to be my medicine. Not only does it delight me and bring me so much joy, it also soothes my nervous system.

Even if you're not a particularly anxious creature, we are all living in a culture that has become increasingly more distracted, disconnected, and lonely. So many of us are settling for what psychologist and author Francis Weller calls "counterfeit joys"—the hit of dopamine we get when our phone dings or the likes we get on social media—instead of real connection. We all want to feel more vibrant and alive, but we're not quite sure where to even start.

While I am first and foremost an artist and a photographer, I am also a life coach. I love helping people use creativity to move through challenges with more ease, get clarity on their desires, and explore how to make their lives richer and more satisfying. I encourage my clients to become Wonder Seekers so they experience more everyday joy.

I define a Wonder Seeker as someone who actively looks for things that delight them. A Wonder Seeker is curious and kind, vibrant and open-hearted. A Wonder Seeker doesn't step over what's hard, only "look on the bright side," or put on a happy face to avoid feeling what's painful. A Wonder Seeker knows that by turning toward what's difficult, by working with what's true (even when it's hard), we become more brave and resilient.

The best part? We can train ourselves to be Wonder Seekers. We can learn to step out of our ordinary lives—even for just a moment or two each day—to witness the everyday magic. The key is where we put our attention.

WHEN YOU BECOME A WONDER SEEKER . . .

- You will experience more gratitude for your life, just as it is, without changing a thing.
- You will notice more beauty in the world.
- You will begin filling your life with more color.
- You will be oriented toward kindness—both to yourself and to others.
- You will create a habit of scanning for the good.
- You will be delighted more easily (and others will find you more delightful!).
- You will wake up your creative spirit and begin expressing that well of creativity inside you.

This book walks you through simple activities that straddle the worlds of creativity and mindfulness. You don't need to be an artist or identify as a creative person to do the activities in this book. They are designed to be fun, easy, and accessible.

WHERE WE PUT OUR ATTENTION MATTERS.

And what we pay attention to grows. So if our intention is to grow our joy and live happier lives, we need to practice putting our attention on what's good.

It seems important to mention that I am writing this during a pandemic. We have been sheltered in place all summer now, barely leaving the walls of our apartments for months on end. There is massive social justice upheaval, fires raging, and tremendous uncertainty in politics and the economy. People are anxious and afraid. Who am I to talk about wonder and joy at a time like this?

But I think this is where the rubber meets the road; difficulty is exactly where and when we need to tend to our joy the most.

You will notice that the chapters of this book span a pretty wide definition of wonder. All the aspects of our lives are woven together—everything from our relationships with ourselves, to our loved ones, and to our connection with the natural world and our relationship with spirit (whatever that may be for you).

I want you to know that this book is meant to be full of serendipity. You can pick it up and choose an activity at random. You can read it cover to cover. You can do the prompts by yourself or team up with a wonder buddy and complete the activities in tandem.

Finally, I want you to know that being creative doesn't mean you make art all the time, although you might. It means reaching for that well of creativity inside you and using it on behalf of your aliveness and joy. Ask yourself questions. Be willing to experiment. Step into the softer, brighter world of possibility and imagination and see what's been waiting for you on the other side.

Andrea Scher

BERKELEY, CALIFORNIA
2020

CHAPTER 1

THE WONDER OF

Nature

WHEN I CONSIDER MY MOST VIVID MEMORIES OF WONDER, they are usually out in nature. I think of the first time I saw the night sky on a camping trip and couldn't believe how many stars there were. I think of the harvest moon rising over the hills, big and amber. I think of the plumes (of what I thought was smoke) floating by me on a lake, only to discover they were tiny spiders traveling en masse across the water. I think of the joy that erupts inside me every time I see a rainbow.

WONDER LIVES IN THE BODY.

It's a visceral, wide-eyed wow of surprise, delight, and pleasure. It's a full-body yes to life. It is an appreciation of beauty and a reverence for the natural world.

Last fall, my friend Laurie Wagner and I co-led a creative workshop in Oaxaca, Mexico. In addition to the daily writing and photography lessons we planned, we also curated some hands-on excursions with artisans in the area. This included visiting an artist who made traditional Oaxacan black pottery, another who taught us about making tin hearts, and a cooking lesson where we made squash blossom quesadillas and roasted pasilla chiles to make the most glorious smoky salsa.

The highlight of the trip, however, was taking the group to learn natural dyeing techniques from a master dyer named Juana Gutiérrez Contreras. She and her family, who are all textile artisans, live in Teotitlán del Valle, where they work to preserve the indigenous Zapotec tradition of using plant and insect dyes to make handwoven rugs and other textiles.

The first things I saw when we arrived were dozens of prickly pear cacti hanging up in rows. They looked illuminated from within, like they were glowing. Upon further inspection though, I could see that insects were living

on those cacti and that the white glow was actually the cochineal bug attaching itself to the plant. Juana showed us how this tiny ash-colored bug, when squished, turned the most brilliant crimson and could be used for dyeing. She crushed it in our friend Alicia's hand for us to see. It looked bright and alive, like blood in her palm.

I walked around with my camera photographing everything around me— the hanks of wool in a gorgeous spectrum of color, the vats of indigo, the glowing cactus, pomegranates dripping from trees, and Juana herself, with her long dark braids, magenta ribbons woven into them.

I WAS BREATHLESS FROM ALL THE BEAUTY.

When we travel, it's a bit easier to be wide-eyed and awake. We aren't stuck in our habitual ways of doing, being, and seeing. We have an intention (whether conscious or not) to experience something new, joyful, and exciting. But we can learn to see our regular world with fresh eyes too. We can get present enough to marvel at the beauty right here, right now. It's a slight pivot of our attention, but a meaningful shift in consciousness.

I know that joy is on the other side of this waking up and noticing.

This chapter offers activities that will help you make that pivot. We will practice orienting toward simple beauty, putting our attention on the small, sensual details of our everyday world. We will notice the color of the sky each day and the slant of the light in the late afternoon. We will go on treasure hunts to the grocery store and pick up rocks and feathers that glimmer in our path. We will create a *noticing* practice—where we don't rush by things in favor of getting somewhere or accomplishing more on our endless to-do lists—but instead, take life in more slowly and consciously.

We will understand that to be awake in this life, to notice all the riches right here, is everything. That without taking pleasure in the small things, we are not able to appreciate the fullness of our lives as a whole.

1. Take a Curiosity Walk

WONDER MOST OFTEN FINDS US THROUGH THE SENSES. We stand inside a redwood grove and look up, marveling at the beams of light coming through these gigantic old trees. We smell the night-blooming jasmine and are heady with the sweetness. We hear a thrum, a vibration of energy we can't identify, until we turn to see a hummingbird at eye level staring back at us.

It is through our bodies that we experience wonder. **This is how wonder lands us in the moment, fully present.**

I've been experimenting with unplugging on my walks. Instead of listening to podcasts or books, I remind myself to tune in to the sounds of the place—birds rustling in the trees, my shoes tapping along the ground, dogs

barking in the distance. I tune in to the smell of pine and eucalyptus. I notice that I actually *see better* when I'm not lost in the world of my thoughts (or taking in media), and I notice more beauty. I am more available to be where I actually am—*in this body, in this moment.*

In this way, the walk is more like a moving meditation, a chance to settle my mind and have a break from the noise of the world. Most exciting for me, perhaps, is that I usually come away with more clarity and new ideas after these walks, probably because my intuition doesn't have to compete with other things for my attention. I'm more available to listen.

A curiosity walk is the perfect way to get embodied and wake up your creativity. It doesn't have to be long or anywhere in particular. It can be on a suburban sidewalk or a woodsy trail. You can do it on your lunch break or at the magic hour. This is an experiment in using all the senses to take in your environment.

It's noticing juxtapositions of color and tiny details you might never have paid attention to.

It's about listening to the sounds of that particular place.

It's touching the bark of the tree and smelling those strange little flowers that you're not even sure have a scent, but what the heck? We're just getting curious.

ON MY WALKS I HAVE NOTICED THAT . . .

- The plum blossoms smell like corn tortillas.
- There are clouds in puddles (that look like portals!) if you see them at the right angle.
- The beads of water that collect inside miner's lettuce bobble around in the most whimsical way if you play with them.
- Cats watch me through the windows of houses.

Get out there and look, listen, and sniff around! I want you to be like a detective, taking in all the details you can through all your senses.

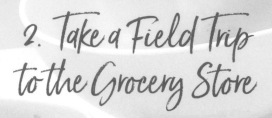

2. Take a Field Trip to the Grocery Store

WHEN MY SON BEN WAS LITTLE, we walked through the produce aisle one day and he pointed to a dragon fruit, a spiky, magenta number with apple-green scales (like dragon eggs!).

"What is *that*?" he asked and reached for it. "What's *inside*, Mama?"

Since I had no idea, we decided to take it home and find out.

It was exciting for both of us to not know what was inside. And we couldn't have been more surprised and delighted when we opened it up.

"It's like poppy seed ice cream in a hot pink candy shell!" we practically shouted.

Miraculous. Ben scooped out spoonfuls, and we assessed the flavor, crunching the tiny seeds between our teeth.

"Hmm . . ." We both considered it thoughtfully, like judges on one of those cooking shows.

"It tastes like a really bland kiwi," he finally said.

But neither of us cared about the taste. To be in this place of shared curiosity and discovery was really the wonder of it. We could hardly believe that dragon fruits exist! And since they do? Well, the world is indeed a magical place.

Your assignment is to find something mysterious in the produce aisle. Something that inspires curiosity.

Find something you've never tasted before (or more than one thing!) and have a tasting flight of unique flavors. Next to try on my fruit list are rambutan, mangosteen, fresh lychee, and kiwano!

The spirit of this exercise is to experience delight in something new, such as trying foods you've never tasted before. My hope is that it brings you a sense of wonder about the world and all the flavors in it (without having to leave home!). Something that expands your sense of what's possible— reminding you that there is always more to discover, to be curious about, to experience, and to love.

your findings

....

....

....

....

....

....

....

....

mangosteen

3. Drink Moon Water

I'VE ALWAYS BEEN ENCHANTED by a ritual that an old housemate would practice during the full moon. Before she went to bed that night, she would leave a bowl full of water on the kitchen table, right where the moon shone in the window. She would let it fill up with the moon's energy all night and then drink it the next morning.

This housemate had a lot of rituals that fell into the witchy camp, but this is the one that always resonated for me. Instead of asking her exactly how she did it, I decided to create my own version.

What I love about this ritual is that it helps me feel more connected to the rhythm of the natural world and has me take a moment of quiet to consider my wishes and gratitudes for the month—a beautiful moment of reflection and intention setting. Many believe in the magical properties of the energy of the moon itself, that you are literally drinking in the moon's energy. But I don't think you need to believe that in order to get the benefits of the ritual, which, to me, are more about taking a moment to check in with yourself, tune in to your desires, and feel appreciation for all the goodness in your life.

I don't do it every single month, but it's always a wondrous thing when I do. Sometimes, I even put it in mason jars and gift the magic water to friends. I tell them to think about their wishes and intentions while they drink it and know that they are supercharged with the moon's energy. This is always met with surprise and delight!

Here's a simple way to do this ritual (modify as you wish!):
1. Find a pretty bowl and fill it with water.
2. Put the bowl outside (a place where it won't be disturbed) or near a window where the moonlight can flow in.
3. Close your eyes and infuse the water with whatever wishes and blessings feel most potent for you right now. What would you like to create more of in your life? Know that the moon energy will supercharge your intentions.
4. In the morning, drink the magic water!

4. Go on a Wonder Date

A WONDER DATE is an outing, a field trip, even a simple picnic in the backyard—but with a clear intention of experiencing wonder. It could be sitting on the deck watching the stars, visiting the modern art museum, or heading out to see the sunset. It's really about setting an intention to experience beauty, delight, and inspiration. It certainly doesn't need to be outrageous or expensive. Just a simple declaration—"Let's have a wonder date!"—is enough to orient ourselves toward some everyday magic. It also doesn't have to be with another person. Wonder dates are great to do by yourself.

I called a friend recently to invite him on a wonder date.

"Hey, Michael! Would you like to have a wonder date with me today?"

He had no idea what I meant but immediately responded, "Of course! How could I say no to that?"

jellyfish that looks like a diamond!

I explained a bit more. "I'm thinking we can meet in Point Reyes, go to the beach, have buffalo-milk soft serve from that one market, and whatever else we can think of that would delight us. If it's later in the day, maybe we can see the sunset or the stars! Or if that one farm will let us visit, maybe we can see the baby goats? I just want us to spend the day looking for joy and magic."

For me, it was a bit of an experiment. What if I set a clear intention to experience wonder? Would I experience more of it on this particular day? Would I be more awake to it? I think planning a wonder date is *actively putting yourself in the way of wonder*. It increases your chances of experiencing it because your attention is there. It helps you train your eyes to other magical moments in your everyday life you might be missing.

I also noticed that wonder is not transactional. You can't go to a beautiful place and immediately experience wonder. It doesn't work that way. Wonder, like joy, is something that arises in you. You could be in the most beautiful place in the world—on a beach in Hawaii—and be totally crabby. *It's too hot here. There are too many bugs. Too much sand.* Wonder often catches us by surprise. There is a deeper mystery to it.

For example, when Michael and I had our wonder date, the beach was beautiful and the ocean was turquoise and stunning. But the enchanting moments were tucked into the day in unexpected ways—like when we were cold and buried our hands deep in the warm sand and let out a big sigh of happiness: "It's like taking a hot bath!" we exclaimed.

It was the moment when the pelicans flew in perfect formation over our heads; it was the translucent jellyfish strewn all over the wet sand that looked like diamonds; it was the moment when we said goodbye and our eyes met in deep gratitude for the joy of the day and our friendship.

What's an enchanting place that you'd like to share with someone else? For me, there is a camera obscura in San Francisco that is totally mesmerizing. It's set right next to the ocean, and the building itself (with the words "Giant Camera" written on the outside) functions like a pinhole camera. Inside, you find a big concave white table (shaped like a contact lens) that reflects the scene happening outside, which happens to be the rocks, the ocean, and the beach. The disk spins slowly, revealing a 360-degree view of the outside . . . so the image becomes more like a video image. It is one of the most magical things I've witnessed, and I love to bring people there any chance I get.

Although I go to lots of places by myself, I believe our joy is amplified when we share it with others. If I am by myself and see a rainbow, for example, my first impulse is to shout to anyone within listening range, "Isn't it beautiful?!" I think it's a natural impulse to want to share beauty with others.

SOME WONDER DATES I'D LIKE TO HAVE:

- Sleep in a glass dome in the desert and see the night sky.
- Watch the moon rise.
- See the dahlias in Golden Gate Park in San Francisco.
- Collect sea glass.
- Have an outdoor dinner with twinkly lights.
- Look through a telescope at the stars.
- Go to a sound bath (one of those places where you lie on the floor and the healer plays singing bowls).

WHAT WONDER DATES COULD YOU GO ON THIS MONTH?

WHO WOULD YOU LIKE TO INVITE?

WHAT WOULD YOU FIND ENCHANTING?

HOW COULD YOU INCREASE YOUR CHANCES OF EXPERIENCING MORE BEAUTY AND MAGIC?

5. Measure the Blueness of the Sky

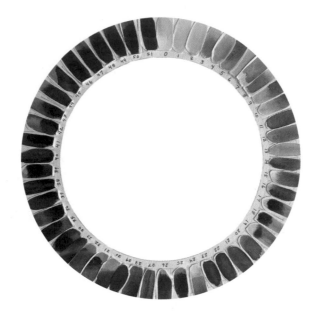

THIS IS A HOMEMADE CYANOMETER! And it measures the blueness of the sky. Cool, right? The idea was invented in 1789 by a Swiss physicist named Horace Bénédict de Saussure, who was interested in measuring how the color of the sky changed at different altitudes. He wanted to answer the question that has plagued humans since the beginning of time: Why is the sky blue?

The original tool itself fell out of use, but the artifact remains. I find it so beautiful—elegant in its humble purpose, pleasing for its color. To use it, just hold the colorful circle up and see what blue matches your sky that day.

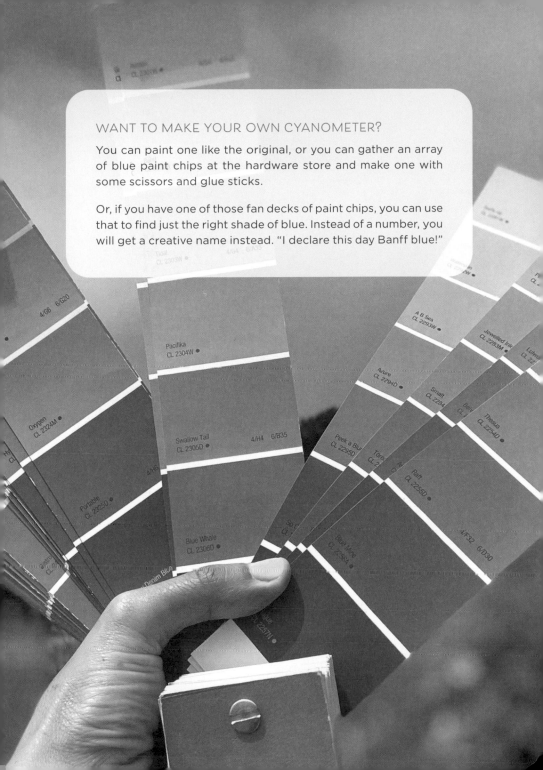

WANT TO MAKE YOUR OWN CYANOMETER?

You can paint one like the original, or you can gather an array of blue paint chips at the hardware store and make one with some scissors and glue sticks.

Or, if you have one of those fan decks of paint chips, you can use that to find just the right shade of blue. Instead of a number, you will get a creative name instead. "I declare this day Banff blue!"

TOO BLUE TO MAKE A CYANOMETER? I'VE GOT YOU COVERED.

As I was creating my own cyanometer out of blue paint chips, I was having a rough weekend. The pandemic was getting to me. The months of sheltering in place, distance learning for the kids, a family friend dying of COVID, all the uncertainty and collective pain was flattening me.

As I looked at the little wheel I was making, I considered how blue I felt and wondered if I was making a *blues*ometer instead—something that measured (and named) the varying blues of my heart. I started naming each color in a kind of free association, going around the wheel in a progression from dark blues (hollow, anxious) to lighter blues that felt more hopeful. I created it over a series of days, as I moved in real time around the feelings wheel myself. It felt good to locate myself on the wheel, an artful way to track my progression.

When I show this to people, they immediately want to locate themselves on the wheel too. It's strangely comforting to name what we are feeling, especially when it's nuanced, as emotions generally are. Having the right language helps us feel seen and understood, even to ourselves.

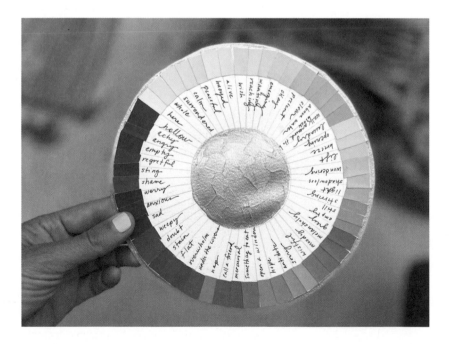

Here's a fun way for you to create your very own feelings wheel. First, grab a pack of colored pencils, markers, or paint. Next, go around the wheel, choosing which colors you feel correspond to each feeling. Keep going until you have filled the entire wheel!

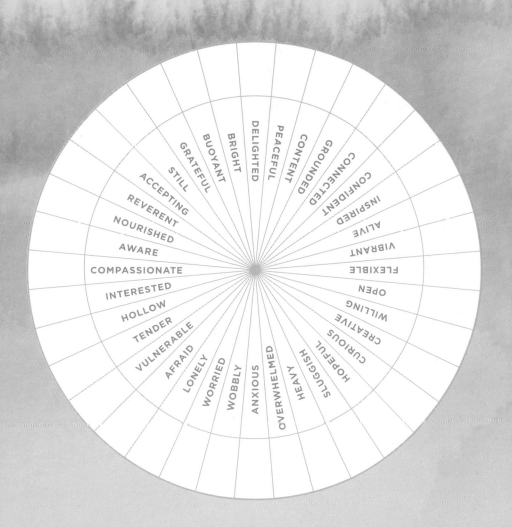

6. Cloudspotting

IF I'VE DONE MY JOB WELL AS A MOM, my children will forever roll their eyes and remember me as someone who pulls over to the side of the road and says things like: "Is that a heart in the clouds?" "Holy smokes!" "Whoa . . . do you see how they look like jellyfish today?" "Wait, I just gotta stop real quick and take a photo, sorry!"

That's right. I'm a shameless cloudspotter! And I invite you to be one too.

And guess what? It turns out we are in great company. Did you know that there is a Cloud Appreciation Society with more than fifty thousand cloudspotters from all over the world? These people are cloud nerds like me, taking photos of clouds each day and identifying the different types. Learning about this group made me realize how many kindred spirits are out there!

Let's make a habit of noticing the clouds each day.

HERE ARE SOME THINGS TO LOOK FOR:

- Do you see any shapes in the clouds? Hearts? Dragons? Birds? Angels?
- Are the clouds puffy like cotton balls? Or do they look more like feathers?
- Are there lots of clouds? Or is there just one little puff?
- Do you see any shapes in the negative space between the clouds?
- Can you find a cloud in a puddle?

CLOUD *bingo*

DINOSAUR	BEAR	SEATED BUDDHA	BLURRY	COTTON BALLS
RIPPLES LIKE WATER	ELEPHANT	ROCKET SHIP	STRIPES	SUNSET CLOUDS
HEART IN THE CLOUDS	ANIMAL SHAPE	NO CLOUDS AT ALL	A SHAPE IN THE NEGATIVE SPACE	A BIRD
AN ANGEL	ONE LONELY PUFF	CLOUD PUDDLE	FEATHER	JELLYFISH
COTTON CANDY CLOUDS	A FACE IN THE CLOUDS	UFO	A HOLE IN THE CLOUDS	AN EYE IN THE SKY

7. Create a Wonderscape

JUST LIKE A TABLESCAPE (an artistic arrangement of objects on a table), a wonderscape is an artistic arrangement of wondrous things you've collected! It can be natural things like rocks and shells or man-made things like small toys, marbles, or spools of thread.

Where a tablescape functions more like a decorative centerpiece, a wonderscape invites curiosity and interactivity. It wants people to play with it, ask questions, and feel a sense of wonder about it. It can be quirky or sentimental. Nostalgic or spark a memory. Each item tells a little story.

Wonder Seekers tend to be the best kind of scavengers. We collect little bits of beauty as we move about the world. A wonderscape is a way for us to display them and artfully arrange them.

HOW TO MAKE A WONDERSCAPE

1. Gather your treasures.
You might already have some fun things around the house to add to your wonderscape! I found heart-shaped rocks, sea glass, sand dollars, and a tiny jar of glitter to put in mine. You could also head out on a walk with the intention of bringing home some treasures. Things like bottle caps, pine cones, colorful leaves, and seed pods are great to look out for.

My friend Elke has a wonderscape full of vintage spools of thread, thimbles, and feathers. Anything that brings you a spark of joy is perfect for a wonderscape!

2. Find a vessel for them.
You can put your treasures on a shelf or in a bowl or spread them out on a pretty serving platter. It can be seasonal (perhaps made of natural things you collect on your daily walks) or something you build over time.

My friend Rachel's wonderscape hangs on the wall in one of those vintage letterpress drawers. It's full of treasures her young daughter finds when they are out and about, little toys and other curiosities.

3. Share it.
If you'd like to photograph your wonderscape and share it with the Wonder Seeker community, just hashtag your photo with #wonderseeker #wonderscape. So excited to see what you create!

WORKSHEET

What Are Some Memories of Wonder in Your Life?

for me...

The smell of night-blooming jasmine.

The first time I heard a live gospel choir on a Sunday morning.

When someone told me that you could fry an egg on the sidewalk if it was hot enough.

The first time I saw a shooting star.

When bats were flying around at twilight while we were camping.

That time it hailed out of nowhere, and we ran outside with a mason jar to catch the hailstones.

**Take a moment to list as many memories as you can here.
Here are some prompts to get the wheels turning:**

THE FIRST TIME I . . .

WHEN I LOOKED UP AND . . .

THAT TIME WE WERE . . .

I COULDN'T BELIEVE THAT . . .

IT WAS SO SURPRISING TO DISCOVER . . .

IT WAS JUST PLAIN DELIGHTFUL WHEN . . .

WHEN I WAS ABOUT FIVE YEARS OLD I . . .

WHEN I LEARNED THAT . . .

THE FIRST TIME I HEARD . . .

MY EYES GOT WIDE WHEN . . .

CHAPTER 2

THE WONDER OF

You

IN MY HIGH SCHOOL, THE BEST ASSEMBLY OF THE YEAR was always when the hypnotist came. The hypnotist was an older man dressed in a suit (like a magician) who would somehow get a group of classmates to do silly things in front of the whole school. As the audience laughed and cheered, the students onstage were always completely serious and unselfconscious (rare for high school) and followed the hypnotist's every command. I was enthralled. How did he do it?

One morning during my senior year, I heard that the hypnotist was on campus looking for volunteers to be in the performance later that day. My hand immediately shot up. I needed to know what the heck happened up there!

A group of about thirty of us were led into a portable classroom and were told to sit at a desk with our eyes closed. He led us through a relaxing meditation and then gave us some suggestions: "Your right arm is getting lighter and lighter. It is like a helium balloon, so light it is floating into the air. . . ."

The kids with their arms highest in the air, about ten of us, were chosen to be in the performance. Apparently, the height of my arm matched my enthusiasm! But I worried as we marched onto the stage in the auditorium. *Was I really hypnotized? Or was I just faking it? Maybe I just did what he said because I was being good. . . .I don't feel hypnotized.*

But there we were, in front of the entire school, seated in little chairs ready to embarrass ourselves. When I had seen these assemblies before, they often involved students clucking like chickens onstage. I prayed we wouldn't have to do that. For a moment, I regretted that my curiosity had gotten the best of me.

But suddenly he was speaking to us. "You are a Russian ballet troupe! We are so excited you are visiting our school! Why don't you show us what you've got?"

I love dancing, I thought as I pirouetted around the stage. *I'm such a good dancer!*

Then his voice again after we sat down: "This is your pilot speaking. We are climbing to an altitude of ten thousand feet, and it's getting very cold in the cabin." We all started shivering in our chairs.

It went on like this for a while.

Then the hypnotist walked up to me and whispered, "Do you have any back problems?"

I shook my head.

"Good," he said, and took my hand, leading me to the front of the stage. He had already placed two chairs there, about three feet apart, facing each other. He placed me between them and put the microphone down so only I could hear him. "You are a steel bar, Andrea. You are made of steel. Straighten up, you're a steel bar!" I straightened my body and nodded.

He laid my body between the chairs, with my feet resting on one chair and my head on the other. How on earth could he have done that? I just remember repeating to myself over and over again, *I'm a steel bar. I'm a steel bar. I am made of steel.* At one point, I could feel him pressing on my stomach, showing everyone how strong and steel-like I was.

But get this. Apparently, when I thought he was pressing on my stomach, this six-foot-tall man had actually *stood on my stomach*. (I was a steel bar after all, so what's the big deal, right?) Oh, and he jumped up and down on me. (I was probably five feet tall and one hundred pounds at the time.)

"What happened?" I asked my friends after the assembly. I never felt hypnotized but seemed to do everything the hypnotist told me.

"It was crazy!" they replied. "He was jumping on you! How did you do that?"

(I think we can all agree that this story would never happen in schools today!)

Decades later, on a layover in Querétaro, Mexico, I met a man who told me he was a hypnotist. "Do you do school assemblies?" I asked excitedly, "and make the kids do silly stuff onstage?"

He nodded. Then I described my steel bar experience.

"Was that real?" I asked him. "Did that really happen?"

He smiled knowingly. "We are so much more powerful than we realize."

This is a message I've needed to hear so many times in my life. I needed to hear it when I was going through infertility. I needed to hear it when my son started having seizures. I needed to hear it when my marriage ended. I needed to hear it when I stepped onstage for the first time to give a talk.

Maybe you need to hear it too. Maybe you need to hear it right now.

YOU ARE SO MUCH MORE POWERFUL THAN YOU REALIZE.

We have so many negative thoughts that get in the way: *You're doing it wrong. You're failing. You should be doing more. You should be different. . . .* But really, we are so powerful and tender all at the same time. They are inextricably tied—the softness and the strength.

This section of the book is about the *wonder of you*. Your superpowers, your gifts, the wisdom of your body, and so much more. We don't need to step over what's painful or uncomfortable. In fact, experiencing your whole range of emotions is what carves out space for more joy.

Your body is a wonder; your heart is a wonder. This chapter is about celebrating the unique, imperfect beauty that is *you*.

8. Discover Your Superpowers

DID YOU KNOW THAT YOU HAVE SUPERPOWERS? That just like the comic book superheroes, you too were bestowed special gifts and strengths that make you uniquely you?

I don't mean the ability to fly or become invisible. . . . I'm talking about the everyday kind of superpowers, like the way you're always able to find gems at the thrift store. Or how you can explain complex things in simple ways that everyone can understand. I'm talking about the way animals are drawn to you or the way you know exactly how someone is feeling, even when they are across the room.

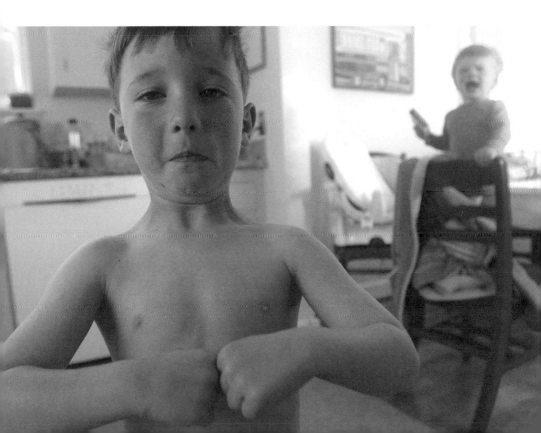

Our superpowers are our gifts. They are the unique strengths that make us who we are. They are what we bring to the party every time, no matter where we go.

THEY ARE THINGS LIKE:

- I connect people.
- People feel safe with me.
- I know how to take a leap.
- I'm a great storyteller.
- I always choose the best gifts.
- I remember everybody's name.

Discovering my superpowers has allowed me to step more fully into my authentic self, without apology and without shame. And that ripples out into everything I do.

Here's a great example. When I first started teaching photography workshops, I thought I had to be a technical expert. I thought I needed to be able to walk into any lighting situation and know exactly what shutter speed and f-stop to set my camera to. I thought that to be a "real photographer" meant that I could answer any question a student threw my way.

But here's the truth: I've never been great at shutter speeds, fancy lighting, or the more technical aspects of taking photos. My eyes always glazed over when someone tried to explain these things to me. I couldn't stand all those years of printing in the darkroom. My superpower (and joy) is taking portraits in natural light, making my subject feel comfortable in front of the lens, and drawing out their essence. My superpower is my attention to color and beauty and telling a story that feels authentic. My genius is in the ease I bring to the party.

When I got married and we got the prints back from the wedding (people were still shooting film back then) I was blown away that every shot was exposed perfectly. I asked my dear friend Ryan, a photography professor who loves the technical stuff, how the photographer was able to get everything exposed so flawlessly given the different lighting situations throughout the day.

"How is that even possible?" I asked him.

He looked over the prints, smiled, and said, "Do you really want to know?"

"Yes!" I said.

"She put it on P."

"What?!"

"She put it on the Program setting."

"No! Really?!"

"Yes. Cameras these days are so sophisticated, they are actually smarter than we are sometimes. Use your tool, girl! You will likely get perfect exposures every time on P."

THIS WAS REVOLUTIONARY INFORMATION FOR ME.

At first I felt like I was cheating. *Really?* I thought. *I can just put it on P? Is that legal?* But the permission to put it on P allowed me to put my attention on the things that really mattered to me—the story, the light, the expression of my subject. It helped me be more playful and connected. It helped me to lean into my unique gifts and amplify those. It also took away that shame I had about not knowing all the technical mumbo jumbo. I've had my camera (mostly) on P ever since.

When I talk about superpowers, it's not the cartoon version. It's not about wearing a cape or being bulletproof. In fact, it's just the opposite! We are exquisitely vulnerable creatures who have incredible gifts to share—things that, when named, can be celebrated and amplified.

And unlike cartoon superheroes, you get to have a lot of powers! Look for the things that come easily to you, that bring you joy. For some reason, we tend to value struggle in our culture. We undervalue ease. I want to orient you toward the things that are most natural for you. You may not recognize them as superpowers because they come so easily, but these are the ones we want to shine a light on.

This exercise is going to help you identify some of your superpowers!

I'm excited to see what shows up for you, what surprises you. Be broad and bold. From the sublime (sometimes I have precognitive dreams about people I love) to the ridiculous (I have a superpower of picking perfect avocados).

What do you bring to the party? What do you bring with you wherever you go?

To get you started, circle the ones that resonate most. Then add your own!

circle

You are a connector. You love to connect people to each other and/or people to resources.

You are a storyteller.

You bring humor wherever you go.   *add*

You bring the real. Those intimate, deep conversations seem to always happen when you're around.

You know how to organize, to create systems, to help people simplify their lives.

You are the resident therapist. People always call you when the you-know-what hits the fan.

You bring the fun, the party, the energy, the shake-your-booty. Things are always more fun when you are around.

You bring the best food.

You bring beauty. From the way you dress to the way you decorate a table, you value beauty and know that life is better when there is more of it around.

You are great at celebrating others.

What are your superpowers?

WHAT DO PEOPLE COME TO YOU FOR?
(To organize their closet? For relationship advice?)

WHAT COMPLIMENTS DO YOU GET ON A REGULAR BASIS?

WHAT DO YOU FEEL ENDLESSLY CURIOUS ABOUT?

WHAT ARE YOU FREAKISHLY GOOD AT?

WHAT FEELS LIKE BREATHING TO YOU (BUT IS HARD FOR OTHERS)?

ARE YOU BEGINNING TO NOTICE SOME THEMES?
WHAT THREADS ARE YOU NOTICING?

9. Let Others Appreciate You

HOW GOOD AT BEING APPRECIATED ARE YOU?

For example, when someone gives you a compliment, do you deflect? Brush it off? Think that they are exaggerating? Would you rather be the one doling out the compliments?

Receiving a compliment is something I've had to practice. Years ago, I promised myself that if someone ever acknowledged me or complimented me, I was not allowed to diminish myself or brush it off. I was only allowed to say a sincere *thank-you*. This practice has helped me stay present and really receive the gift being offered. (It has also helped me feel more confident.)

This might not sound important, but it is. There is power in seeing ourselves clearly and honoring our unique magic. And if you're having trouble nailing down your superpowers, this exercise is going to help.

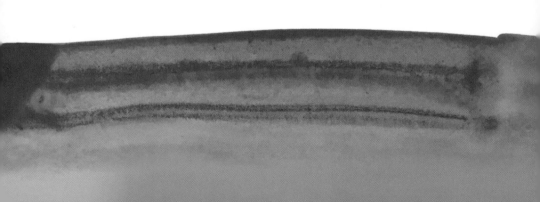

Here's what we're going to do.

You are going to send the following email to five people you love and trust. (I know this sounds scary to some of you, but I urge you to get a bit uncomfortable. If it feels easier, just send it to one person to begin!)

To:

Subject:

```
Dear [Loved One's Name],

I'm reading a book called Wonder Seeker, and our challenge today
is to interview people in our life about our strengths and gifts.

Would you be willing to answer these questions for me?

1.  What are my strengths? Gifts?
2.  If there was one word you would use to describe me, what
    would it be?
3.  What is my superpower?

Short and sweet answers are just perfect!

Thank you in advance,

[Your name]
```

When you get your responses back, take your time reading them. Notice what comes up for you as you take them in. Notice if there is any resistance or if you are telling yourself stories like *She's exaggerating*, or *Well, she's just trying to be nice.*

If you are having trouble receiving these appreciations, go a bit more slowly. Breathe. Trust that what your friends are sharing is truly how they see you.

Do you notice any similar threads? Is everyone commenting on your smile? Or your ability to make them feel at home? Add those to your superpowers worksheet and let yourself take it in as much as you can! Letting others appreciate you is a powerful capacity to build. Getting good at it is a super-power in and of itself.

I AM LARGER,
BETTER THAN
I THOUGHT;
I DID NOT KNOW
I HELD SO MUCH
goodness.

–WALT WHITMAN

10. Choose a Superhero Name

OKAY, FRIENDS. Now that you've captured some of your superpowers, it's time to choose a superhero name! This name will function as a kind of alter ego—the wisest, bravest part of you that always knows what the highest good for all is.

A few years ago, when teaching a class about everyday magic, I asked everyone to choose a superhero name. I have always loved the thrill of using my superhero name at cafés and restaurants and having a superhero self to draw upon for courage. I wanted my students to have this experience too! Plus, it's fun.

I chose the name *Zee*, a name I had heard when I was a kid. I liked the sound of it. Powerful. Creative. Short and sweet. I liked that it was a name and also a letter of the alphabet.

When I had my students look up the origins of the names they chose, I did the same. I saw that Zee was a nickname for an actual superhero from the sixties named Zatanna Zatara. And her superpower? My jaw dropped when I read it: everyday magic! Whoa.

YOUR TURN. YOUR MISSION TODAY IS THIS:

1. **Choose a superhero name.** A name you've always loved. A name you wish you had. A name that sounds . . . *superheroic!* It could be a derivation of your current name or a completely new creation. If you're not sure, just try one on for a week.
2. **Look up the origin of the name.** What's the meaning? I'm a total geek about name origins. When I looked up Zee, it felt like a secret message from the Universe. What does your name want to tell you?
3. **Use it at a café or a restaurant.** If they write it on your cup (or on a receipt from your order), take a photo and share it with me: @andreascher on Instagram with the hashtags #wonderseeker and #superheroname.

57

Your Superhero Identity

I love your superhero name!

Now let's go a little deeper with your superhero persona. We are going to flesh out the origin story of your superhero self. We all remember Superman's story, right? And how the green substance from the planet Krypton was the only thing that could hurt the Man of Steel? Well, let's understand your superhero's kryptonite (what drains her energy and weakens her special powers), and let's explore how she serves. Here is Zee's origin story.

SUPERHERO NAME: Zee

HER GIFTS: X-ray vision, magic, manifesting, sees beauty everywhere, storyteller, healer, truth-teller.

HER PERSONAL KRYPTONITE IS: Wanting other people to like her. Not wanting to outshine anybody else. Sarcasm. Cynicism. Perfectionism.

HER ATTIRE: Knee-high red boots. Gold wristbands. Black tank top. Tight jeans.

HER MISSION: To wake people up to beauty, to inspire people to be brave, to help people lead more lively, joyous, and colorful lives.

HOW DID SHE GET HER POWERS? Lost her voice through some rough parts of childhood. Mistakenly thought she had to be perfect to be loved. Thought being in a body was not so great and preferred the ethereal realms. Found her voice again through her art and her creative work. Rediscovering her creativity has allowed her to feel whole again, alive, committed to being here.

CURRENT ADVENTURE: Living as a single mom and creating a brand-new life and story with her kids. Discovering powers she didn't know she had. Feeling connected to the Universe in a way she never thought possible. Realizing she is not alone in the world.

Your turn

SUPERHERO NAME:

HER GIFTS:

HER PERSONAL KRYPTONITE IS:

HER ATTIRE:

HER MISSION:

HOW DID SHE GET HER POWERS?

CURRENT ADVENTURE:

11. Find Your Full-Body Yes

THE BODY IS INCREDIBLY WISE. We know this. It has so much to share with us, but we haven't been trained to listen or to be in conversation with our bodies. Our bodies call out to us, but we have forgotten to give them the loving attention they ask of us.

After my divorce, I was terrified to be a single mom. I had never lived alone and suddenly had my own place with two small boys. *How would I afford it? Would I be terribly lonely? Would I be alone forever?*

I noticed some numbness in my right foot one day. I rubbed it and found that it was tingly and painful to the touch. *Strange*, I thought. After months of this, I googled my symptoms (terrible idea!) and got really scared. It suddenly occurred to me to ask my foot what was going on. I closed my eyes, put my hand on my heart, and asked my foot, "What are you trying to tell me?"

I was surprised to hear a small voice in me say, "I'm afraid to move forward."

Intuitively, I responded, "Oh my goodness, of course you are! So am I! We've never done this before, and it's scary. We are grieving. This is hard. But I've got you. We've got this sweet little home, and the boys are safe and good. I'm scared too, but we're going to be okay."

The next day the pain wasn't there. Or the numbness. It never came back.

Since then, I check in with myself often. I put my hand on my heart and ask, "Is there anything you need me to know? What's here today?" Sometimes I just say to myself, "I'm here. I've got you. I'm listening."

Yes!

THE FULL-BODY YES

I worked with an intuitive coach named Juna Mustad for several years as I navigated all the changes in my marriage and family structure. One of the best things she taught me was the full-body yes—a way to connect to your intuition, to include your body in the process, and get a somatic yes or no when it comes to making choices, both big and small.

Here's a little exercise that helps to explain:
1. Close your eyes and imagine that a food that you really, *really* don't like is in front of you. (For me this would be truffle fries.) Now imagine you are leaning toward it, about to eat that food. Notice what happens in your body when you move toward it. Do you feel a contraction in your body? A tightness? Where do you feel it?
2. Now, close your eyes and imagine a food that you absolutely *love* in front of you. Something you find totally delicious. Like a layered chocolate cake with whipped cream frosting. Now lean forward and imagine you are about to eat this wonderful thing. What happens in your body as you move toward it? Do you feel an expansion in your body? Where do you feel it?

This exercise helps you track *your* unique feeling of yes or no in your body. For me, a *yes* feels expansive and my body tends to lean forward. My shoulders open. A *no* for me feels like a tightness in my chest. My head pulls back, and my face scrunches. Visually, it looks like a messy scribble of pencil all over my heart. What about you?

Knowing your full-body yes is your own personal GPS system. It is your intuition speaking through you, through your body—that precious body that always tells the truth.

As women especially, we are natural givers and nurturers. This is beautiful, but we can also burn ourselves out when we get into habits of saying *yes* when we mean *no*. This exercise is a way of getting conscious about what an authentic *yes* is for you. And perhaps even more important, it is an invitation to practice saying *no* when it's not.

Let's go a little deeper:

1. Take out a sheet of paper and make two columns.
2. Write this: "Things I have a full-body YES for" on one side and "Things I have a full-body NO for" on the other side.
3. Write quickly. Write big things and small things. Let yourself be surprised by what shows up.

Practice this with low-stakes situations in your life this week. When a friend asks you out for lunch, see if it's a full-body yes for you. Make a pledge that if it's not a full-body yes, it's a no, at least for now.

As you grow this skill of discernment, you will also be growing your ability to set healthy boundaries, which is an important act of self-love. But you need to know what your truth is before you can speak it. Your body always knows, even if your mind doesn't. You can trust it.

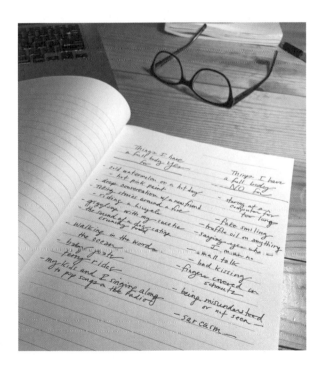

12. Write a Word on Your Body

YEARS AGO, I used to gather on the Oregon coast with an amazing group of creative women—all authors, artists, and joymakers. Our intention was inspiration, community, and fun—and also an opportunity to encourage each other to shine as brightly as possible. We affectionately called ourselves the Lovebombers . . . and there was always beautiful food, love notes hidden all around the house, and artmaking we would do together.

One year, the talented novelist Katherine Center brought her favorite brush and black paint with her for a special project: She offered to paint our bodies (our arms, our hands, our backs, our chests) with whatever words we most needed to hear. They could be individual words, a line of poetry, whatever was meaningful to us.

What unfolded was a surprisingly deep ritual.

When it was my turn, I was surprised by how shy I felt. She asked me what word I wanted, and I stuttered and stammered, resisting the word that kept coming to mind: *lovable.*

Really? I thought. *Does it have to be* lovable? *That's so embarrassing!* Then I started to cry, and finally eked the word out. Okay, *lovable.*

Katherine wrote it over and over across my arm, in big flowy cursive and then in smaller printed type. I saw the word creep over my shoulder and felt the tickle of her brush across my hand. The black paint seeped into my skin, and as those words seeped in, of course the truth of it seeped in too.

Many of us come up with a core story when we are young that we spend our entire lives unraveling. *I'm not smart. No one wants to hear what I have to say. I'm not good enough. My needs are too much. I'm not lovable.*

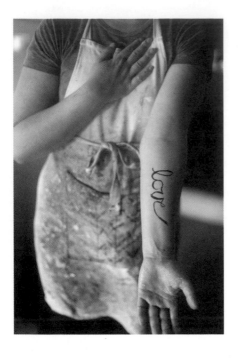

Lovable came to the surface for me (as much as I tried to find a different word!) because in that safe beautiful space, my wisest self wanted to be heard. She wanted to say, *"You are lovable*, sweetie. And if you don't believe me, we are going to have this nice lady write it on your body over and over again until you do!"

Something shifted in me as a result of this exercise. Maybe it was the week with friends, or the loving way Katherine didn't ask questions but just painted the words and let me cry. Maybe it was allowing a vulnerable part of me to be seen. Maybe it was shining the light of compassion on something old and tender that allowed for healing.

If you were to be painted, what words would you choose?

It doesn't have to be the deepest or heaviest thing. It can be something that you value (*courage*), something you want to remind yourself of (*you are powerful*), or maybe a mantra (*let it be easy*). Once you have your word or phrase, write it in marker or paint somewhere across your body. Then photograph it and share it with the Wonder Seeker community by using the hashtags #wonderseeker and #wonderwords.

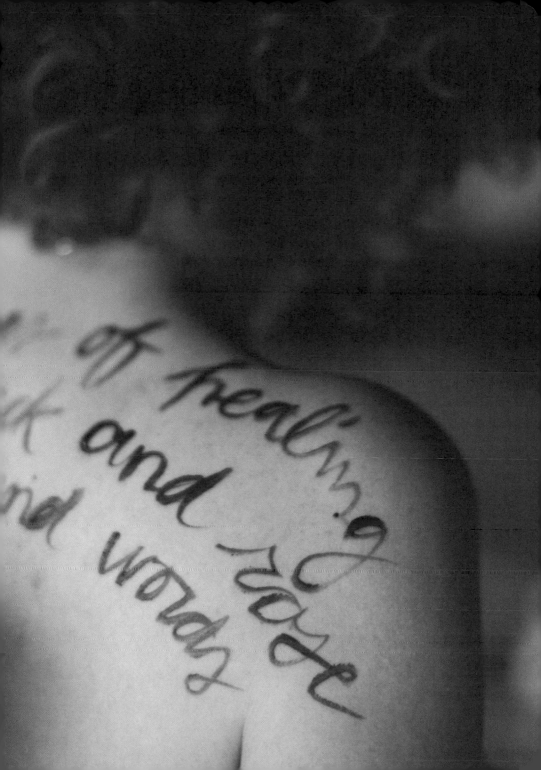

13. Meet Whatever Shows Up with Kindness

WHEN I SAW THE WORDS *GRIEF WORKSHOP 10 A.M.–6 P.M.* in my calendar, I thought, *What the heck was I thinking when I signed up for that?* For years, my friend Carmen had been telling me about Francis Weller, a psychotherapist, author, and grief ritualist. I didn't think twice when I saw he was coming to Berkeley. I just signed up!

But I had so much resistance when the day actually arrived. *I don't have anything big to grieve anyway,* I thought. *I will feel like an impostor.* A few beats later, I remembered: *Your marriage. You need to grieve the death of your marriage.* Oh yeah, that.

We do so much to distract ourselves from loss. We make ourselves busy. We numb our pain with food and alcohol. We scroll mindlessly on social media so we don't have to feel our sorrow. We do this mostly unconsciously.

As I walked into the meditation center where the workshop was held, I felt the grief begin to bubble up in my chest and the tears begin to pool in my eyes. It was as if my body was already thanking me: *Thank you for letting me be here. Thank you for putting your attention on me.*

I found myself feeling so grateful that I had finally been invited to inhabit and express my sorrow somewhere. I no longer had to suppress it or contain it anymore.

During the ritual, Francis spoke about how we have undigested sorrows . . . and that grief is a capacity we can build, a skill that we can strengthen. It requires courage and vulnerability. It requires a willingness to be with things as they are. He said, "Grief might be the remedy that heals us. Grief is wild. It's feral. And when we touch it, we are *alive*."

Put your hand on your heart and ask yourself, "Is there something I haven't been feeling that I need to feel right now? Is there something you need to tell me?" Listen for the answer. Notice if you feel tender just asking the question.

When I ask myself these questions, I often notice an ambient anxiety or sadness. It might be faint, just a hum of a thing in the distance. But as I stay with it longer, I grow more curious. I might ask, "Are you afraid? What are you afraid of?" And then, when I hear the answer, I say, "How can I help?" or just "Ah, I get it. I'm with you, sweetie."

If we want to live a life full of wonder, we need to be willing to meet whatever shows up in us with kindness. Whatever we push down or push away corrodes in us, gets sticky and mucks up the works. Allowing all our emotions to do what they were designed to do—move through us—carves out space for us to be present and awake for the moment.

Now you try it.

Put your hand on your heart and do a little check-in. Ask yourself, "What's here right now?" "Is there anything I need to feel?" "Is there anything you need to tell me?"

This simple, hand-on-heart check-in is a great way to stay connected to your spirit, to listen deeply, to not step over what might be needing some attention in you. Whatever you find there, meet it with kindness.

14. Make a Time Capsule

THE FIRST TIME I EVER HEARD ABOUT A TIME CAPSULE was from an extraordinary math teacher in junior high school. In addition to teaching us math, he also taught us about creative play and that learning can happen in unconventional ways. He had a legendary loft in his classroom where students could sit if they arrived early to class and seats from vintage cars sprinkled around the room. He had a joyful, mischievous spirit.

One memorable time, a student left the room to go to the bathroom, and he had us rearrange all the furniture and pretend nothing happened when they returned. Another time when someone went to the restroom, he told us that he would be doing an "optical illusion" later that day. "Just be sure to pick the *wrong* answer!" he told us.

As promised, he drew two lines on the chalkboard and asked, "Which one is longer?"

Everyone chose the shorter one. We watched the one student totally bewildered but quiet.

Then the teacher drew two more lines. "Okay, which one of these is longer?"

Again, everyone chose the shortest line. After a few rounds, the person couldn't take it anymore and spoke up. We all cheered for them! Then we had a really interesting conversation about how much courage it takes to resist going along with whatever everyone else thinks and what it means to trust ourselves.

As you might imagine, it was rare that students skipped his class.

My favorite day though was when he had us pull out a sheet of paper and answer a list of questions privately. They went something like this:

- *What do you love to do?*
- *Who do you have a crush on?*
- *Who are your friends?*
- *What's important to you?*
- *What books do you love?*
- *What is your dream?*

70

We sealed up our answers in an envelope. He then told us that he would collect the envelopes (promising to never open them) and would deliver them back to us five years later, when we graduated from high school. This was an entire *lifetime* away for a seventh-grader.

I'm sure most of the students forgot about this list, but I didn't. I contacted him during my senior year of high school and volunteered to help him distribute the envelopes. I remember being shocked to see that my secret crush from the seventh grade had become my high school boyfriend and first love (and one of my dearest friends to this day).

So in the spirit of my beloved teacher and creative play, I invite you to make a little time capsule too!

HERE ARE A COUPLE OF OPTIONS (OR FEEL FREE TO INVENT YOUR OWN!).

Option #1: Write a love note.
Take out a nice sheet of paper and your favorite pen. Light a candle maybe. Sit quietly and write yourself a note from your highest, most loving self. This might make you feel shy, but that's okay. Sometimes it helps me to imagine my spirit guides and angels are writing a letter to me. Just imagine the most loving and wise voice you can conjure up telling you all your wonderful qualities. And trust me, you will be amazed by what comes through.

Option #2: Write a letter to yourself from a year in the future.
Everything went exceptionally well! And the year was full of dreams come true, joyful adventures, and big love. *Who did you meet? What new experiences did you get to have? What dreams did you get to make real?* Write this letter in the past tense, as if it all unfolded beautifully. (This is a fun way to manifest all sorts of goodness in the coming year!)

When you're finished with either (or both!) letter, seal it in a self-addressed, stamped envelope (for privacy) and mail it to a friend. Someone of course who is willing to mail it back to you in a year! If you can find a buddy to do this with, you can trade envelopes and mark your calendars for a year out. Truly, it feels like a miracle when it lands in your mailbox.

CHAPTER 3

CREATIVE

Magic

AS GROWN-UPS, WE DON'T ALWAYS LET OURSELVES PLAY!

Play is a thing we have largely forgotten, deeming it a waste of time in a hurried, hyperproductive world. Maybe we think it's something for children or impractical. Maybe it's because we live in a culture that doesn't value it, instead praising hard work and struggle as worthy of respect.

But play is an essential part of birthing creative ideas, finding joy, and feeling fully alive and present. Not to mention, it's so much fun!

IT TAKES
COURAGE TO SAY
yes
TO REST AND PLAY
IN A CULTURE
WHERE EXHAUSTION
IS SEEN AS A
STATUS SYMBOL.

–BRENÉ BROWN

Play is also at the core of our creative spirit. If we want to feel fully alive, we need to feed the creative creature in us and allow her to play and imagine and move her body in joyful ways. It doesn't need to be like playing board games or throwing Frisbees at the park. Play can look like crossword puzzles with your morning tea, dressing up for a costume party, or making something with your hands. Really, it's anything that isn't "productive" in the traditional sense.

I have a recurring dream where I am somewhere tropical and beautiful and I am packing for my flight home. That's when I realize that I never made it to the beach! I never swam in the ocean! *Oh no!* I will say in my dream. *How did I forget that?! Is there time to go now?* But there is a flight to catch, and it's a long way to the airport, and I see the blue of the water out the window, and I feel a deep ache of longing and regret.

Elizabeth Lesser says it perfectly in her book *Broken Open*. She says there are two kinds of people. Those who are afraid to die and those who are afraid they will die without having truly lived.

I would place myself firmly in that second camp. And for me, having truly lived includes play.

My friend, poet Maya Stein, says it so beautifully here:

Years ago, I had an argument with someone about whimsy. She couldn't understand why I would ride my bicycle from Amherst, Massachusetts, to Milwaukee, Wisconsin, towing a manual typewriter behind me to collect stories from the strangers I met along the way, when there was so much more "important work" to be doing. I did it anyway, and there was a day, in the middle of a back road in Indiana, my little bike tow trailer rattling behind me with the Remington Ten Forty secure in its case, when I felt, quite suddenly and viscerally, like I was exactly where I needed to be. In one exquisite moment, my heartbeat aligned with the heartbeat of the world. I'll never forget the way my body held that sensation of congruence, the glee that erupted from my cells. I rode in the fullest throttle of freedom I'd ever known. And I remembered the argument about whimsy from months before and thought to myself, *There is no more important work than this.*

This chapter celebrates the kind of play I call creative magic. It's playing with words and color. It's finding faces in your food. It's writing poetry from paint chips. It's gathering leaves and arranging them in a spectrum. It's calling on that well of creativity inside you, not with the expectation of making great art, but in service to your aliveness and joy. It's a way to loosen up, slow down, and have more fun. It's part of a rich life, truly lived.

Leitman **LONG STORY SHORT**

SOMETIMES I FEEL LIKE A FOX   DANIELLE DANIEL

LOVE WARRIOR GLENNON DO

JENSEN  HERE WE ARE
FEMINISM FOR THE REAL WORLD

LEAH PEARLMAN   Drawn Tgether   Uplifting Co
Journey Thro

 Spilling Open  Sabrina

Ellen Bass   Like a Beggar

 CHERI HUBER   WHEN YOU'RE FALLING, DIVE

15. Spine Poetry

NEVER WROTE A POEM BEFORE? NO PROBLEM. ME NEITHER!

In fact, I've always been intimidated by poetry, having only read classical poetry in school, which at the time was totally unintelligible to me. I started appreciating poetry more in my forties, when I discovered contemporary poets like Ellen Bass, Mary Oliver, Marie Howe, and Alison Luterman. For the first time, I discovered poetry could be accessible, could touch me in profound ways, could hold deep wisdom, and could tell stories.

And I didn't know *I* could write a poem too (as someone who doesn't fancy themselves a poet!) until I saw this exercise going around on Instagram, book-spine poetry. It is a type of "found poetry," which means you don't need to use your own words and phrases, but the ones you find in your environment are fair game. In this exercise, use what you find on your bookshelf!

This idea started gaining momentum back in 2012 when writer Maria Popova (inspired by artist Nina Katchadourian's Sorted Books project) started writing poetry this way. I love the accessibility of it (anyone can participate as long as they have a few books to spare) and that you get to see the poem in three dimensions, not just on the page.

You ready? We're going to write a poem using the titles of books as lines of verse.

1. To get warmed up, pull approximately five to eight books off your shelf and start playing with the titles as lines of poetry.

2. Now arrange them in a bunch of different ways to get the creative juices flowing. Try stacking a set by color and see how the lines interact with one another. Try going alphabetically and see what sort of story emerges. Or close your eyes and randomly grab five books off the shelf. Do you tend to overthink things? Set a timer for ten minutes and use the time constraint to motivate you.

   This is creative play, so get curious and move the books around like puzzle pieces! Eventually, you will see a story or something whimsical emerging.

3. Photograph your poem! And post on social media with the hashtags #wonderseeker and #spinepoetry.

Here's mine (and pictured on previous spread)! If I were to interpret it, I see a snapshot of a woman in the throes of transformation, trying to be brave in love and to surrender to life as it's unfolding.

Long story short,

sometimes I feel like a fox

Love warrior,

here we are

drawn together

spilling open

Like a beggar

When you're falling, dive.

Write your spine poem.

....

....

....

....

....

....

....

....

....

....

....

....

What is it trying to tell you?

16. Leave a Love Note on a Banana

SOMETIMES I LEAVE NOTES FOR MYSELF ON BANANAS.

It started out as something my friends and I would do for each other on our yearly retreats to the Oregon coast. We would leave little love notes (on Post-its) all over the beach house where we stayed and waited for each other to find them. It always felt like serendipity to stumble upon a note, like it was written just for you!

Back home in my kitchen one day, I looked over at my fruit bowl and wondered if I could do the same on a banana. I grabbed a ballpoint pen and wrote my first banana note to myself: *I love you.*

The pen glided perfectly along the smooth texture of the peel, and as the banana ripened, the words bruised in just the right way to reveal the message even more clearly.

It might seem strange that these notes are usually for myself and not my kids or someone else, but I'm learning to get more comfortable with this practice of quirky self-love. Seeing those words of love and positivity reminds me that I've got my own back.

Leave a little note today for yourself or for someone else to find in the house. Or write a banana note when packing lunches to surprise your loved ones. The positive affirmations will feel like magic when discovered!

Not sure what to write? Here are some short and sweet suggestions:
• You are just right. (Or just *ripe* if you like banana puns.)
• Good morning, beauty!
• I adore you.
• You are doing great.
• I'm proud of you.

17. Find a Face in an Unlikely Place

DO YOU EVER SEE FACES IN INANIMATE OBJECTS? Me too! Apparently this psychological phenomenon has a name, pareidolia, and it is a Wonder Seeker's delight. The surprise of finding a face delights me at first, but then I'm amused by the fact that I have a new little friend in my coffee or in my burrito. With my new friends at my side, the world seems a bit more enchanting!

For those of you who see faces in everything—the shower tile, the cottage cheese ceiling, the clouds—this prompt will not be much of a stretch for your imagination. I think we all have the capacity to see the world through creative eyes, but most of us have dulled this impulse in favor of focusing our attention on (seemingly) more practical tasks like answering emails or crossing off our never-ending to-do lists. I'm here to tip the scales!

Finding faces is one way I flex my play muscles on a daily basis. It reminds me not to lose that childlike piece of my heart to the seriousness of being a grown-up. Maybe you've noticed a similar burst of excitement when rolling down a grassy hill. Or doing a cartwheel. Or jumping on a bed. Nurturing this piece of our spirit helps us stay connected to our creativity, to our right brain, and to the part of us that is willing to try new things and see the world anew.

And we're definitely not alone! Did you know that there is a museum in Japan dedicated exclusively to rocks that look like human faces? It is called Chinsekikan (Hall of Curious Rocks), and it apparently houses 1,700 unique rock faces. The photo on the facing page is from my own rock faces collection. If I ever get to Japan, I will bring him with me!

For me though, it all started with Cheese Dog (pictured on the facing page), the Saint Bernard I found in my gorgonzola one night at a dinner party. I gasped when I saw him and proceeded to pass him around the dinner table to all of the guests, who let out shrieks of recognition and excitement. You'd have thought we had seen the Virgin Mary!

Over the years, I have found sad bananas, grouchy lemons, dinosaur clouds, and many other wondrous things!

Your mission is to find a face in an unexpected place.

Look at the shapes on your plate, scan the rocks at your feet, and study the clouds each day (don't forget to look at the negative space between the clouds too). Plus, you can name your new friends! This pickle (with a llama face) above is affectionately named Llamickle.

When you find a face or two, celebrate by photographing them and sharing on social media! Use the hashtags #wonderseeker and #facesinthings and see what faces other people are finding in everyday objects.

18. Extend the Invitation

SO OFTEN, WE ARE WAITING FOR A JUICY INVITATION, for our people to find us, to be plucked out of the crowd and *chosen*.

I wait to be invited to dinner parties.
I wait for someone to invite me to make art with them.
I wait for someone to invite me over to tell stories around a fire.
I wait for someone to call and say, "Can we go on a wonder date together?"

But here's the good news: We don't need to wait any longer. We can be bold enough to extend the invitation ourselves. We can be the ones to say, "I have this kooky idea where we all gather and make crafts together and then we have to give our creation away to another person in the room! Who's game?"

We can create the experiences that we most want to be having right now.

What are you most hungry for these days? How could you give that away to yourself or others? Or what's the silly but delightful thing you want to put out there? What's the fun idea you have that you would love some company in?

At the beginning of sheltering in place, it was my dear friend Laurie's sixtieth birthday and we weren't able to celebrate her in person. As I racked my brain for a good gift, I remembered how much I've always wanted to be part of a flash mob. Especially the kind where they erupt into dance and song and life looks like a spontaneous musical! It occurred to me that I could gather some of her friends and we could do a version of this on Zoom to surprise her.

Over the course of a couple of weeks, we choreographed a hilarious dance routine and then performed it for her on her birthday. She was totally blown away—laughing and crying (tears of pure joy!) the whole way through.

And like all the best gifts, it was a gift to us as well. In a time that felt incredibly scary and uncertain, where we were all anxious, emotionally wobbly, and overwhelmed, this gift for Laurie became the most joyful place to put our attention.

My friends seem to be outrageously good at creating the experiences they most want to be having. For example, during a lonely time in my friend Lisa's life, she decided to stand on the corner of a busy intersection in Oklahoma City and hold a sign that read, "You matter." People honked and waved their appreciation. A few jumped out of their cars just to hug her. It's as if she were offering the world the medicine that she herself most needed.

Another friend was obsessed with a particular cookbook by Heidi Swanson but felt overwhelmed by all the recipes. She gathered a few foodie friends, and every week, each person in the group would cook a dish from the cookbook. They even came up with a contest. Whoever managed to get a selfie with Heidi would win a dinner where everyone cooked for them!

One day I want to have a cereal party with friends where we create a buffet of all the illicit, sugary cereals our parents would never buy for us as kids and have a dinner party with them! We could call it the Buffet of Banned Cereal!

Okay, friends. What's the silly or meaningful thing *you* want to experience? What's the fun idea you have that *you* would love some company in?

19. Levitate

AFTER SEEING THE PIXAR MOVIE *UP*, my boys asked me how many helium balloons it would take to float them into the air. Would ten do it? Maybe twenty? Or would we need hundreds? I can remember wondering the same thing when I was a kid and imagined how fun it would be to fly through the neighborhood this way.

My son Nico and I decided to try it. We got a bouquet of helium balloons and planned to set sail in a meadow at Tilden Park in Berkeley. It was clear we wouldn't actually fly (even to Nico I'm certain), but we loved suspending disbelief and letting ourselves imagine . . . plus, I knew we could make a fun photo op out of it!

We brought my next-door neighbor and dear friend Mati Rose (an artist herself, always up for creative shenanigans!) and we took photo after photo of each of us jumping in the air with the balloons in hand, creating the illusion that we were being floated into the air. This attracted a woman who was already having her photo taken in the meadow. She asked if she could jump with the balloons too. She jumped over and over again in her Hawaiian dress until we got just the right shot. Wonder is infectious!

It makes me think of a conversation I overheard recently on a walking trail near my house. It was a group of kids, about nine years old, discussing the tooth fairy.

"Well," one of them said, "my mom—*I mean the tooth fairy*—used to bring two-dollar bills." She corrected herself quickly, as if she knew it was her mom but wanted to believe in the magic a little bit longer.

The others didn't correct her and continued the conversation about what the tooth fairy brings them. Even though they were old enough to question it, they wanted to live in that world of magic as long as possible.

And this is what I realized Nico and I allowed ourselves to do during our levitation experiment—suspend disbelief just a wee bit longer. We wanted to live in a world where maybe, just maybe, it would work. And we would fly.

Go get yourself a balloon bouquet! Then grab a friend and see if they will step into the magic with you! It's so much fun, and you will get some amazing photos out of it.

After we arrived home, Mati and I wondered what to do with this awesome bouquet of balloons. Was it anyone's birthday? A graduation? We wanted to secretly leave the balloons for someone and make their day—like benevolent balloon bandits!

We considered tying a balloon to each mailbox on our little cul-de-sac, but one balloon looked lonely, so instead we tied the entire bunch to our neighbors' house, the ones who had small children. We tied them up quickly and ran away so they wouldn't see us.

A couple of days later, we got an email from the family. "Thank you for bringing a little magic into our life this week! We saw you two run away after you left them!" They had included photos of their kids playing with the balloons.

"You are so welcome!" we replied. "But we wanted to be balloon bandits! We thought you hadn't seen us!"

The next day, Mati and I received bags of peaches and apricots at our doors. The attached card was signed, *From the Neighborhood Fruit Bandits*. This is how the joy ripples out, friends!

People are hungry for delight, for surprise, for things that put a splash of color and joy into the world again. It helps us believe that the world can be a magical place. One where we can fly with the help of enchanted balloons, where there are benevolent bandits in the neighborhood ready to shower you with fun surprises, where people are kind and generous.

And who knows what the Fruit Bandits might do for someone else as a result of our simple, playful gesture? I do know that every time we pass by this family on our street and wave, there is an extra nod of connection and joy. Even though we don't know them well, we are forever bonded by the sweetness of these moments of play we created together.

20. Write a Paint-Chip Poem

I'VE BEEN OBSESSED WITH PAINT CHIPS for decades. It's a visceral experience for me. Every time I walk into a hardware store, that gorgeous spectrum of color pulls me in like a magnet. I take each strip and hold the array of greens, pinks, and tangerines, and my heart swells. What is it about color that makes an artist's heart light up?

When I went on my first date with my now ex-husband, Matt, he happened to have a stack of paint chips in his bag. He was renovating an old Victorian at the time, and as he was riffling through his backpack, the paint chips fell out. He saw my eyes light up.

As we thumbed through the paint chips, we noticed how extravagant the names of the paint colors were: Second Honeymoon, Perfect Privacy, Harvest Mist, Salty Sound, Daydream. . . .We created a game where we chose a paint chip randomly and had to begin a story using that paint color. The next person would choose another paint chip and continue the story using that color name.

It went something like this:

"Megan's Eyes" were so beautiful that whenever she looked at a man, they would be temporarily blinded.

(Next person chooses a color)

"Smoked Salmon" was the only fish they could eat together.

(Next person chooses a color)

"Seedless Grape" was what she always had for dessert, and she always made her suitor peel them for her.

This put us into a flirty bout of hysterics.

When we got married, our invitations were designed to look like paint chips (a nod to our first date) with the information about the wedding on each line of color. The RSVP cards were Mad Libs–style fill-in-the-blanks that were also styled to look like paint chips of course.

Paint chips are also a fun way to write a poem—especially if you've never written one before or you feel intimidated by poetry in general.

Here are some simple instructions:
- Go to the hardware store and gather some paint chips. They are free! But if you feel self-conscious, you can tell the clerk what you're up to. "I'm writing paint-chip poetry!" you can say. I am always met with a curious kind of delight.
- Using the names of the colors, find words and phrases that call out to you and feel evocative and resonant. Cut those chips out.
- Arrange them in a variety of ways until they fall into poetic verses that speak to you.

Together, under the stars,
Texas summer.
Sour apple, cabbage
rose, summer pear
Spontaneous
Dark moon, bright future.

I interpret the paint chips almost like reading tea leaves. After I create the poem, I decide what the poem is trying to tell me. Matt and I eventually separated and divorced (after many sweet years and two awesome kids), but in the pieces above, I think it spoke to my romantic notions of love at the time. A second chance at love.

Paste chips

Your poem

....

....

....

....

21. Grow the Lexicon

HAVE YOU EVER HEARD THAT EXPRESSION "a murder of crows" or "a parliament of owls"? I just learned that these are called *collective nouns* and was excited to discover that there are hundreds of them! They are wonderfully colorful, conjure great visuals, and read like poetry. Below are some of my favorites:

A circus of puffins
A glory of unicorns
A harem of seals
A scold of jays
A shimmer of hummingbirds
A galaxy of starlets
A bloat of hippos
A sneak of weasels

Let's invent some new ones. Maybe one day, they'll end up in the lexicon!
Here are some I came up with:

A pillow fight of feathers
A carnival of toddlers
A bonanza of clovers
A wiggle of puppies
A glamour of hipsters

HERE, GIVE IT A TRY! FILL IN THE BLANKS BELOW.

A _____ OF PICKLES

A _____ OF PACKING PEANUTS

A _____ OF OCEAN WAVES

A _____ OF COFFEE BEANS

A _____ OF HUGS

A FESTIVAL OF _____

A HOWL OF _____

A SHINE OF _____

AN AWAKENING OF _____

A WONDER OF _____

A CONSTELLATION OF _____

A WORRY OF _____

AN ENCHANTMENT OF _____

WHAT WAS YOUR FAVORITE COLLECTIVE NOUN THAT YOU CREATED?

CHAPTER 4

WONDER

Spotting

AFTER YEARS OF BEGGING MY PARENTS, I got my first real camera for my twelfth birthday. I was over the moon and couldn't wait to have my friends over for a fashion photoshoot–themed birthday party. I slathered my girlfriends in lip gloss, used a hair dryer to blow their hair like I saw in magazines, and fashioned a shower curtain into a backdrop. I quickly discovered how much I loved taking portraits.

One evening, while my dad was grilling in the backyard, I noticed the nozzle of the garden hose sitting on the railing of our deck. I'm not sure I had ever noticed it before, and most definitely had never considered it beautiful. But in this moment, I literally saw it in a new light. I didn't know it at the time, but it was the golden hour (the time of day right before sunset), when *everything* looks beautiful: fire hydrants, mailboxes, discarded candy wrappers on the ground—everything. The light is warm and diffused, shadows are long, and there is a summery glow in the air. I ran inside to get my camera.

A few weeks later, when I got the prints back, I was astonished by the photo of the garden nozzle. I had somehow managed to capture the beauty of the light in that moment and made this ordinary object look elevated.

I felt like I had discovered a secret of the Universe. *There is so much beauty people pass by without a thought!* I decided to make it my business to notice unlikely beauty, not just the pretty sunset or the great view but also the everyday things that we would rarely register. I wanted to capture those with my camera. I wanted to be a person who saw beauty everywhere.

I know that underneath the mess everything is marvelous. I'm sure of it. I know it because I feel so marvelous myself most of the time. And when I feel that way everybody seems marvelous . . . everybody and everything . . . even pebbles and pieces of cardboard . . . a matchstick lying in the gutter . . . anything . . .

From then on, photography became my superhighway into the marvelous.
When I see pink petals against the fog, my heart leaps a little. When I look
through the viewfinder, I get a zing in my belly just before the shutter goes
click. Even on the hardest of days, the beauty of the world can pull me
back to the present. I can literally see the world through a different lens—
one that honors the miraculous. The bright green sprig of life bursting
through a crack in the sidewalk, the way the white petals fall like confetti
onto concrete, the impossibly long lashes of my boys.

Underneath the mess, everything is marvelous. I'm sure of it.

For many years (while going through a long season of depression), gratitude
practices eluded me. I had heard that writing down what you are grateful
for each day in a journal could help lift you out of depression. But I didn't
feel grateful. I just felt *ashamed* . . . for all that I was blessed with and how
sad I still felt.

What I was still able to do, however, was appreciate beauty. And this saved me.
The glittery beads of dew on the grass, the clouds I found in puddles of water,
the inside of a dandelion. They saved me from being swallowed up by grief.

So after years of kicking myself for not keeping a gratitude journal, I realized
that I already had a gratitude practice of my own! It's just that it was visual
and happened while I was walking around taking photos. With my camera in
hand, I was moving through the world with a different kind of consciousness.
I was carrying the questions, *What is beautiful about this moment? What
is interesting? What can I appreciate?* It brought me back to the now, back
to what I could touch with my hands and away from the chaotic swirl of my
thoughts. It helped ground me in what is right here. This moment. This
pavement. These flowers. This sky. This light.

THE NEGATIVITY BIAS

There is science to support why my photo walks had such a big impact on me. Have you ever heard of the negativity bias? It essentially means that negative things will have a greater effect on us than neutral or positive things. Dr. Rick Hanson, renowned psychologist and bestselling author of *Hardwiring Happiness*, says, "Our brains are like Velcro for bad experiences and like Teflon for good ones." For example, we will obsess over the one mean comment we get on a Facebook post and barely take in all of the kind ones. Or we will skip over all the praise during a work review and only hear that one bit of criticism. So why do we do this?

Our brains are still wired for survival, a holdover from a time when we needed to scan for predators for fear of being eaten. And even though there is no such danger of this kind in most places today, our brains are still hardwired to search for what could be a threat around us.

In order to level the playing field and increase our chances of feeling more joy, we need to train our brains to also scan for what's *good* and to orient our minds toward what's working in our favor. We need to get out of what Dr. Hanson calls the red zone (fight, flight, freeze) and get our nervous systems back into the green zone of resilience and calm. Actively putting our attention on beauty is one of the easiest ways to deepen this neural pathway and train our brains to feel more joy and well-being.

However, just like seated meditation, this takes practice. But I'm excited to offer another way into mindfulness if you have a hard time sitting still! This next section is a kind of treasure hunt—a series of photo prompts that will help you create a habit of scanning for puffy clouds, for tiny beautiful things, for riots of color, for magical light so you can take a moment and see the unlikely beauty all around you.

Just put on your wonder goggles and grab your phone (or camera) to begin!

22. Find a Heart on Your Path

I HAVE FOUND HEARTS in sticky blots of gum on the sidewalk, in the soy sauce droplets on my sushi plate, in many a slice of olive bread. I have found heart-shaped rocks, heart-shaped leaves, and heart-shaped clouds in the sky.

I've decided that each encounter with a heart-shaped anything is a sign from the Universe telling me I am loved. That everything is going to be okay. That no matter what, I am not alone.

Find a heart on your path this week.

You can find them in the crook of a tree, spray-painted on fire hydrants, in your cappuccino, and on your dinner plate. Once you set an intention to find them, you will see them everywhere!

Then repeat after me:
I am loved. Everything is going to be okay. I am not alone.

I am loved. Everything is going to be okay. I am not alone.

23. A Riot of Color

THIS IS YOUR INVITATION to look for bright color, oceans of color, kaleidoscopic color, riots of color! One of my favorite places to do this is at the dry cleaner's. In my city, the dry cleaner usually has a tailoring service as well. When you walk in, you will see sewing machines with big spools of thread displayed on the wall. I always ask to photograph them! And even though they eye me curiously, they always smile when I show them the results in my camera.

Other great places to look for riots of color:
- The flea market or vintage shops.
- The paint-chip wall at the hardware store.
- Fields of flowers on road trips.
- A bowl full of hard candy at your grandmother's house.
- The walls of markers, paints, and pencils at the art store.
- The farmers market.

Capture it with your camera and if you post to social media, use the hashtags #wonderseeker and #riotofcolor so we can find you!

24. Stroll at the Magic Hour

WANT TO KNOW MY SECRET as a portrait photographer? I schedule all of my sessions for the magic hour! This is the time of day (about an hour before sunset) when the air is still, the shadows are long, the light is diffused, and everything looks warm and dreamy.

Photographing portraits is especially beautiful at this time of day for all the reasons described above! It softens the face (no hard shadows) and adds a summery glow to your subject. Being out at this hour feels like a delicious celebration of light, sunshine, and the beauty of the natural world.

Take a stroll at the magic hour and see how the most ordinary things come alive for you. If you want to cultivate a greater appreciation for ordinary beauty, magic-hour strolls will be your secret weapon.

25. See the World Upside Down

WHEN WAS THE LAST TIME YOU WERE UPSIDE DOWN? If you're having trouble remembering, you're not alone—most adults can't remember! But we did this intuitively as kids. We would hang upside down on the monkey bars, the crooks of our legs supporting our weight. We would stand on our heads and do somersaults. We would hang over the edge of the bed and chat.

We would also climb trees to see the world from up high. We would lie down on our backs on the warm pavement and look up at the sky. We were naturally drawn to seeing the world from different vantage points.

And here's what I know: It's good for our creative spirit to see things from different perspectives. It stretches us, helps put us in a curious mindset, and allows us to think about things in new ways. It helps us stay supple and playful. Plus, it's fun.

Today, we're going to do one of my favorite silly activities from childhood. Chin faces! Do you remember having your friend turn upside down, drawing eyes on their chin, and having them talk to you? I just tried it out with my sweetie, and guess what? It's STILL hilarious.

Your instructions are very simple.
- Turn your child, your sweetheart, or whoever you can get your hands on upside down and attach some googly eyes to their chin. (Or draw eyes on their chin.)
- Put glasses on them, draw a nose (optional), and cover their actual nose and eyes with a cloth of some kind.
- Allow hysterical fits of giggles to ensue.
- Photograph your chin-face friend and share: #wonderseeker #chinface.

26. Arrange Your World by Color

WHEN I WALKED INTO Adobe Books in San Francisco back in 2004, I was astounded. The entire bookstore had been organized by color! It turned out to be an installation piece by artist Chris Cobb and a team of volunteers who spent an entire night rearranging all twenty thousand books in this bookshop. What resulted was an experience of pure wonder and joy. It was like stepping through a magical portal, an alternate reality where life was more beautiful and hopeful. How is it that this one unexpected twist on the way we normally organize a bookstore could result in something so mesmerizing?

Years later, after my divorce, I moved into a little treehouse apartment in the redwoods. I wanted the house to feel like a sanctuary for me and my boys, so I filled it with as much color, art, and twinkly lights as possible. As I set up a bookshelf in the living room, I remembered the bookstore project and began organizing my own book collection by color. It's such a simple change, but it brought me joy every time I walked into the room. Give it a try and see if it brings some extra delight to your home.

Already arranged your books by color? Try this one instead.

1. Choose a random color.
2. Walk around your house and collect every object you can find in that color. Junk drawers are a great place to look!
3. Place the objects in parallel (and/or at ninety-degree angles) and photograph all the objects. The technical term for this is *knolling*. A white background is nice for the color to pop but not required. Share it with the Wonder Seeker community: #wonderseeker #colorcollection.

27. Search for Soft Color

SOMETIMES I FORGET how beautiful the softer tones can be. I am usually drawn to the Day-Glo pinks, the hottest of turquoise, the more saturated and kaleidoscopic stripes of my seventies childhood. But when I saw these farm eggs at the grocery store, I marveled at their quiet beauty.

At first, I found myself favoring only the blue ones and wished there were more.

But then I realized that the blue eggs only stood out because of the company they were in. Each tone, each color added something to the harmony of the composition. The lone chocolate-brown egg and the white eggs would look quite ordinary on their own, but together, they are so perfect and necessary.

I trust there's a metaphor in here somewhere.

Capture some soft color today, whether you see a pale peach wall with peeling paint, or a handful of sand against the sky of an almost setting sun. Or go to the grocery store and find some pretty eggs to capture. Turns out they are all good eggs.

28. Let's Blend In

RECENTLY, I was in line at the grocery store and the woman in front of me had to dash back and get one more thing. When she returned with a bunch of beets, I immediately noticed her beet camouflage: bright green top, dark purple pants, and earthy brown sandals.

"Oh my goodness," I exclaimed. "You match that beet perfectly! Even down to your shoes! Can I photograph you?"

She was amused by my excitement and kept looking back over her shoulder, smiling at me as she left the store.

I am pretty much always attuned to color, which is why I noticed this woman so quickly! But I invite you to put your color goggles on today and see if you can find a way to blend in to *your* environment. Or find someone else that matches their environment!

This is a prompt that might take you some time to pull off. Just keep it in mind as you move through your days. Maybe you stumble upon a pink wall and realize it's the same shade of pink as your sweatshirt! Or maybe you are dressed the same color as the fur on your dog. Start noticing the color palette of each place you go and how you can blend in.

Then take a photo and share with your fellow Wonder Seekers: #wonderseeker #blendingin.

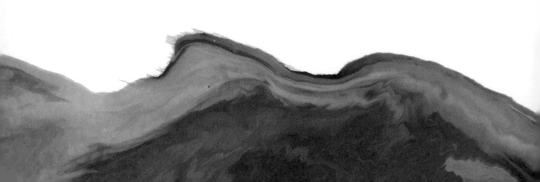

29. Find Beauty in an Unlikely Place

MY LOVE FOR URBAN PHOTO WALKS started in San Francisco. There is so much rich (and unlikely) beauty to discover in the city—discarded couches people leave on the side of the road, faded signs on the sides of brick buildings revealing old advertisements, bright orange traffic cones juxtaposed against a blue sky.

There is a French expression I've heard, *jolie laide*, which translates as "ugly beautiful," or "unconventionally beautiful." And I find those things some of the most intriguing to photograph. There is a tension here, a beauty that isn't obvious.

Writer and poet Deena Metzger says, "Poetry is beauty and ugliness side by side."

And I would agree. Things aren't particularly interesting when they are just beautiful. I am drawn to the imperfect beauty of the cracked sidewalks, the peeling paint, the stained, and the disheveled.

Real life is messy and imperfect. It's temporal. It fades and wears. It dies and decays. If we can find beauty in this too, then we have a superpower that will help us hold all of life's imperfections with much more grace.

Your Wonder List

Write down ten things you would love to see/do/experience that would put you in the way of wonder.

Think of this as your bucket list for wonder! Here are some prompts to help:
Where have you always wanted to go?
What have you always wanted to see?
What experience have you always wanted to have?
What experience might feel like magic?

HERE ARE SOME THINGS ON MY LIST:

- Experience the northern lights (aurora borealis).
- See fireflies. (I have never seen them!)
- Participate in the ancient Hindu festival called Holi where people drench each other in brightly colored powder.
- Photograph the fall leaves in New England. (I just learned this is called leaf-peeping!)
- Go on a moonlight hike at White Sands National Park.
- Witness a miracle.
- See bioluminescent algae.
- Be inside a rainbow. (Is that even possible?)

WHAT'S ON YOUR LIST:

CHAPTER 5

THE WONDER OF

Connection

THE NIGHT BEFORE I MET MY DEAR FRIEND ERIC, I was having a sleepover at my friend Laura's house. As I drifted off, I started talking to her in my sleep. "I'm going to make a new friend tomorrow!" I declared with delight.

"Good for you!" she replied, humoring me, not quite sure if I was coherent.

Sure enough, the next day I was writing in my journal at a café, and I noticed a handsome man sitting near me reading a book. I tried to get his attention. "So . . . ," I began. "Whatcha reading?"

He looked up for a moment, answered quickly, and went back to his book. I persisted, somehow sure I was supposed to talk with him. He was like a magnet, pulling me closer.

"This is my favorite place to write in my journal," I said, flashing my notebook full of photos and drawings. When he saw the artwork, he got more curious and his eyes met mine. I'm not sure how I finally succeeded in getting him to talk to me, but within about twenty minutes we had made plans for a date that very night.

After about three weeks of dating though, he broke up with me. I was a little crushed, but I also knew he was making the right call. Then he asked, "Do you want to know why?"

I nodded.

"You didn't ask me any questions. All you did was talk about yourself!"

I was mortified but also confused. "But wait, I shared all this juicy stuff about myself, thinking that was an invitation for you to share. Like a back-and-forth thing. I thought you must be the most boring person in the world! You didn't tell me anything about yourself!"

This was a huge aha moment for me. I had no idea there were such radically different styles of relating to someone. I had grown up in a household where asking questions was on par with *prying in people's business . . .* and it was rude. But here was someone who thrived when someone expressed curiosity in him, who needed the jumping-off point of a question as an invitation to share. Some simple questions would have opened the doorway to his heart.

Though we did not end up being a couple, we did continue to be friends and have been for almost twenty-five years now. And because of Eric, I learned how to ask good questions! And this has made me a better listener, parent, and friend.

When I trained as a life coach back in 2005, I learned even more about the importance of (and the art of) asking powerful questions. There are questions that open up people's hearts—that allow for creativity and possibility and insight—and ones that can shut the whole party down. For example, when you ask someone a "why" question, like "Why do you like the show *The Bachelor*?" it can feel like a judgment, like the person needs to defend their position. But if you ask instead, "What do you love about *The Bachelor*?" it feels more spacious and like an invitation to share.

Several years ago, when I was going through a particularly hard patch of my divorce, I put out a call on my blog (*Superhero Journal*) for support. I have been blogging since 2003 and have shared really openly about what was happening in my life, even if it was a bit messy or hard. My community has always been right there to catch me . . . and since I had hit a kind of rock bottom emotionally (and could not seem to get my head above water), I asked the blog community for some kind words. When Eric saw my blog post, he gave me a call.

I burst into tears when I saw his name come up on my phone. Coincidentally, he was going to be flying into San Francisco the very next day and offered to come see me in Berkeley. The joy of his friendship and the serendipity was like a double dose of love—from both him and the Universe.

When he arrived, he hugged me, and we chatted for a bit outside the restaurant where we were going to have lunch. But then his face got more serious once we were seated. He placed two small pads of paper on the table.

"Fill these out before we talk, okay?" he said, and then went up to order for us.

I looked at the pads. It was a letter he had written, from me to him, that began this way: "Dear Eric, This is how you can love me today. (Check all that apply!)" Then there was a checklist of items that I could choose from, a kind of multiple choice of ways he could love me. I just needed to check the boxes that sounded best.

I was floored. Who was this guy? And how was he such a ninja at asking the right questions and teaching me about how to love people better?

After a cheeseburger and lots of tears (both his and mine as we shared stories), I felt better. I felt connected to Eric. Connected to my okayness in the world. Connected to the truth that if I could manifest a friend like him, who could love me this way, then there was no limit to what I could create in my new life as a single mom.

This chapter is about the magic that our connections with others bring us and how being creative (and intentional) about how we relate to others leads to more depth and joy. Learning how to ask questions (and to listen deeply) changed my life and the quality of all my relationships. My hope is that this chapter will inspire you to connect in more creative and interesting ways with the people in your world!

Dear Eric,
This is how you can love me today.
(check all that apply!)

- ☒ Listen
- ☒ Listen really, really well.
- ☒ Create opportunities for laughter.
- ☒ Let me cry on your shoulder.
- ☐ Drop nuggets of philosophical yada yada.
- ☐ Avoid dropping nuggets of philosophical yada yada.
- ☐ Remind me of the things I know to be true
- ☒ Let our conversation go wherever it wants to go, whenever it wants to go there.
- ☐ Let me vent and process some hurt without you getting all sentimental/sappy and your voice getting all whispery and breathy.
- ☐ Keep me from processing any hurts — I'm so tired of talking about them right now.

Please read below —
I may have written exactly how you can love me today — or it's possible I might tell you something to supplement the list above.

Once again the Universe brings you into my life with the most incredible timing. What a treat to see your smile today.
Love, Andrea

Catching hail in a jar with my nephew!

30. Ask Someone about Their First Memories of Wonder

WHAT ARE SOME OF YOUR FIRST MEMORIES OF WONDER?

This is one of my favorite questions to ask people. They usually pause, get a faraway look in their eyes, and then a smile will creep across their face when they share. When I asked this on Facebook recently, the most beautiful thread emerged:

Andrew O. Dugas
I remember being outside (when I was very young) in the moonlight and seeing my moon shadow. Amazing. My shadow at night, cast by moon.

Jen Toal
I was super tiny and holding my mom's hand as we checked out my new "room" in a place we would be staying. The walls were a super pale purple that I was instantly smitten with. I still remember asking Mom what color it was and the way her answer of "lilac" seemed poetic and perfect to me.

Tracy Arbuckle
The first time I saw the ocean (I was nine), I felt such awe and exhilaration, I turned cartwheels up and down the shoreline!

Cami Shockler
I was five or six and I witnessed an Irish setter give birth to a litter of puppies in a closet. I watched as she removed each sac from each baby. I was in a state of wonder and disbelief for days. I knew there was something bigger than me at play. At six I also recall a relative passing away and observing how all the people reacted as a whole. I knew then time was finite and it filled me with wonder.

Sasha Wizansky
I was in high school in the Boston area, and one night it was snowing. I snuck out after midnight and was the first person to walk through the snow in my neighborhood. The night was silent—no people or cars—just me and the new falling snow.

James David Tegeder
Slowly riding my bike, late on a warm windy night before a storm, and smiling in the wind when I really wanted to cry because it was so beautiful.

Leslie Rein
My first "real" kiss, so tender and slow, with the boy I had a huge crush on. (Turns out he had a crush on me too.) It was the most wonderful feeling.

Jen Moore
Being a young girl dancing onstage with my parents' ballet company and being awash in lights and hearing the sound of the audience laughing and clapping for me.

There is a particular sense of joy we get from talking about wonder, from hearing others' memories of magic, the mystery, nature, impossible beauty. It is a gift to both the asker and the person who answers. Usually, people have never been asked.

I encourage you to be someone who asks.

As I write this, it occurs to me that I've never asked my parents this question! Maybe it feels vulnerable or silly or just out of context. But now I have the excuse of this book, so I will.

Who in your life could you ask this question to? Friends? Relatives? People at cocktail parties?

Recently, my neighbors Supriya and Siddhartha invited me over for a socially distant drink in their yard. I asked them if they would be up for talking about wonder, and their eyes lit up immediately. We don't know each other well, and it would have been easy to default to talking about the pandemic, politics, or even the weather. But this one question—*What were your first memories of wonder?*—opened them up. I got to hear stories of them as children and swimming in rivers in India, of meeting each other hiking in the Himalayas, and falling in love and moving to the United States.

This question draws out sacred stories, creates intimacy, and is a way to connect and celebrate this mystery of being human together.

31. Give Something Away

FOR MY FORTIETH BIRTHDAY (years ago now) I decided to do a personal ritual—something powerful for the forty days leading up to my birthday. Inspired by the book *29 Gifts: How a Month of Giving Can Change Your Life* by Cami Walker, I settled on giving something away every day for forty days. According to the book, it could be a material gift, a thank-you note, a genuine smile. . . . The only rule was that it had to be a conscious give, meaning that when you were giving, it was your clear intention at that moment.

- I wrote thank-you notes.
- I gave big tips.
- I let people ahead of me in traffic.
- I bought two loaves of olive bread and kept my eyes peeled for the lucky recipient of the second loaf, who ended up being my yoga teacher!
- I took friends out to lunch.
- I made brownies for all the neighbors.
- I mailed a friend a photo of herself laughing that I had taken years ago.

What it gave me:
It reminded me of my kind heart, my generous spirit, and the abundance in my life. It reminded me that I have *so* much to give every day and that there is no greater joy than delighting others. It has trained me to look for opportunities to give, and it has opened me up to receiving with even more joy and openness.

Soon after my experiment, I walked up to our local produce market and saw a man who had two bouquets of marigolds in his cart. The bright orangey yellow made me smile in delight, and I complimented him on his choice. In my mind's eye, I saw him handing me one of the bouquets and saying, "You should have this. This one is for you"—swept up in the moment.

He didn't. He just passed me by. But wouldn't that have been perfect if he did?

But here's the thing: I walked away from the marigold man, smiling at my little fantasy, and appreciating the innocent way I expected him to give them to me. This is how giving opens our heart.

Your assignment is to give something away:
- A compliment.
- A flower plucked from the garden.
- A hug.

It doesn't matter what it is, just as long as it's a conscious give. Try it for a week. If you love the ritual, keep it going. Give something away the next day too. And the next. Notice if you feel more loving. Or more powerful. Notice if you feel more gratitude, even though you are the one doing the giving.

I love this experiment because the side effects can be counterintuitive. The more I gave, the more rich I felt. The more I gave, the more powerful. The more I gave, the more grateful.

32. The Teeny-Tiny How-To Film Festival

YEARS AGO, I watched a short video of a four-year-old girl teaching viewers how to juggle one shoe. She had found her mom's phone and recorded the whole thing by herself. The charm of the video wasn't her talent (I'm not sure juggling one shoe is a thing!) but her genuine desire to put her voice in the chorus of things. She wanted to teach others something she was excited about! And her enthusiasm was irresistible.

It reminded me that we all have this impulse to share what we love. It's natural to want to teach others about the things that we've mastered, that we're curious about, or that spark our delight and joy.

As I write this, we are all sheltered in place—feeling isolated and emotionally wobbly—but also getting creative with our time at home and wanting to connect virtually. I remembered the video of that little girl and thought, *We should have a film festival where we all teach the world something we are excited about! And it should be only 60 seconds per film, so no one gets intimidated!*

And so the Teeny-Tiny How-to Film Festival was born! I put out a call on social media and got all sorts of incredible short videos (many from kids!) about how to tap a maple tree, how to invent a new language, how to draw an eye, and more. Participants just tagged me @andreascher and used the hashtag #teenytinyhowtofilmfestival so we could all find each other.

So, my friend, what quirky thing could you show the world how to do? What silly thing could you teach us in 60 seconds? If you were to write the tiniest book in the world, what would the title be? *How to . . .*

Record a 60-second video of yourself teaching the world how to do something, anything!

Ideas for things you can teach us:
- How to find a four-leaf clover.
- How to eat chocolate.
- How to flirt.
- How to draw a goat.
- How to be curious.
- How to make coffee.
- How to convince someone to hire you.
- How to carry something on your head.
- How to feed a fish.
- How to do a cartwheel.
- How to apologize.
- How to cry.
- How to be kinder to yourself.

This assignment is designed to:
- Be fun and easy. (Do it on your phone!)
- Stretch you out of your comfort zone.
- Be totally silly. Remember what it's like to be a kid in your bedroom with nothing to do.

Pro tips

- If you are more of a writer, write that tiny how-to book and read it to us on video!
- Use costumes if that helps you get in the mood.
- The video can be less than 60 seconds. No video is too tiny!
- Tag me @andreacher on social media so I can watch your incredible videos!

33. Find a Gratitude Buddy

IF YOU'VE BEEN HANGING OUT IN THE WORLD of personal development for any length of time, you have probably heard about gratitude practices! Things like keeping a gratitude journal (where you list things you are grateful for each day) can go a long way in helping us see our world with more positivity and keeping our vibration high.

These lists train our minds to focus on what's beautiful and good and what delights us in the smallest of moments. They teach us that no matter what circumstances are unfolding in our lives, we can choose where we put our attention.

Even though I know this, it has taken me years to start (and stick with) a gratitude practice of my own. My gratitude journals only last for a few days before I forget to write in them or get bored. But then it occurred to me what might be the missing ingredient: a gratitude buddy! I needed someone on the other end of those lists, listening to my gratitudes each day so I didn't have to feel like I was doing it all alone.

When I considered who would be a good match for me, my new friend Carmen immediately came to mind. We met at a painting workshop in Mexico and had an immediate, sweet connection. Trouble was, we lived far away from each other! I imagined that exchanging the things we were grateful for each day would be a perfect way to get to know each other and stay connected. And it was!

We agreed to email a list of three things each day that made us smile, that lifted us up or brought us joy. No preamble required. No explanations. Just a simple list exchanged. Here's what our lists look like.

TODAY, I'M GRATEFUL FOR:

1. The magnolia tree outside my window that is blooming hot pink, even though it is winter.

2. How I could see Ben with new eyes as he charmed everyone at the dentist's office.

3. Fitting into my jeans.

TODAY, I'M GRATEFUL FOR:

1. A good night's sleep.

2. The hummingbird that paused in front of me, so close I could hear the thrum of its wings.

3. The guy I met who was walking his cat on a leash.

We agreed not to fret if either of us forgets a day (or two or three). There is no need to apologize. The other person simply presses on and sends their list over. This helps me stay in the game, since I am often the person who forgets!

Do you want to try?

Choose someone you want to cultivate a deeper connection with (or someone you want to be in regular touch with). Send them a quick email like the one below!

To: _____

Subject: _____

Hey, friend!

I read about finding a gratitude buddy in a book called *Wonder Seeker*. I love the idea because I have always wanted to start a gratitude practice but have never been able to keep it up! I think having a gratitude buddy sounds more fun, and I thought of you.

The way it works is that we exchange a list of three simple things each day—small things that lifted us up, made us smile, or brought us joy.

No preamble or explanation required, just a simple list is enough! And if one of us forgets for a day (or two or three), there is no need to apologize. The other person just presses on and sends their list over.

I would love to do this with you! I think it will be a sweet way for us to stay connected!

[Your name]

34. Practice Mudita

ONE DAY I WAS FEELING BLUE and logged onto Facebook. Usually, it's a terrible idea, but the first thing I came across was a post from my friend Rama in Los Angeles: "I don't usually toot my own horn," he began, "but I just won Teacher of the Year at my school!" I went on to watch the short video the school had made to celebrate him, and my heart swelled.

I immediately started a new thread:
"I love it when people toot their own horn. My friends don't do it enough! Tell me one thing you are proud of right now. Toot, people! Toot!"

I watched as dozens of people shared their victories:
- "I got an article published in the *Huffington Post*!"
- "I'm having my first art show in SoHo tonight!"
- "I got through another day."
- "I'm home alone with two puking kids and I'm rocking it."
- "I kicked cancer . . ."

A whole range of life experiences in front of me. And with each reply, my heart felt more and more full, a genuine joy moving through me.

And I remembered learning from James Baraz (cofounding teacher at Spirit Rock Meditation Center and coauthor of *Awakening Joy*) that there is a name for this: *mudita*. A Pali and Sanskrit word meaning "sympathetic" or "vicarious joy." It's the genuine pleasure you get from celebrating others. It's the deep joy that finds you when someone you love is happy. It's the pleasure that comes from delighting in other people's well-being.

It also reminded me of something important—that regardless of what's going on in my life, my heart is still good. That my heart *wants* to celebrate others and to feel joy. That my most natural inclination is actually toward well-being—both for myself and others.

In a world where we are prone to not-enoughness—where it's common to go on social media and feel the pain of comparison, jealousy, inferiority . . . it felt so good to allow the successes of others to buoy me, to literally pull me out of a dark place.

THEIR SHINING LIGHTS ACTUALLY ALLOWED ME TO FIND MINE.

Look for opportunities to catch a vicarious hit of joy today. Maybe it will be your child brimming with delight that they scored a goal. Maybe it will be your dog, wildly excited to go out for a walk. Maybe it will be you chatting with a friend and seeing her beam when she talks about her most recent date.

Or, like me, solicit your friends on social media to share something delightful in their life right now, something they're proud of. Notice what happens to your own spirit as each win comes in!

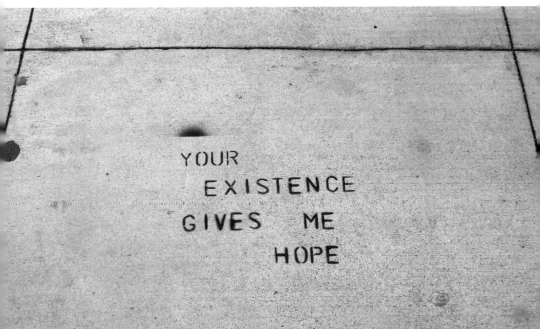

35. Talk to a Stranger

I MISS TALKING TO STRANGERS. I miss the days when people actually chatted with each other on public transportation instead of having their heads bowed in unison, tapping away on screens. I miss the random conversations in the grocery lines before we were all checking our social media feeds.

Once, I was waiting for the bus in San Francisco and an old man turned to me and asked, "What's wrong with your arm? Where'd you get those rashes?"

I looked down at my left arm and replied that we had been having a mosquito problem in our house and that the welts were all in various stages of the healing process.

He pressed on. "Why do you have all those mosquitoes in your house?"

"Well," I began, "it turns out there is a plant in our room with a plastic tray underneath it collecting water. It hadn't been changed in weeks, and a little science project formed. A little pond, you might say. It took us *weeks* to figure this out, but we did, and now the mosquitoes are gone."

Man: "You should treat yourself to a banana split for figuring that out."

Pause.

Man: "We always get down on ourselves and remember all the stupid things we've done. Every once in a while we figure something out and do something brilliant, but we don't usually remember it. If you have a banana split you won't forget."

Okay, so maybe this guy was a little nutty. But it was also kind of genius! And exactly the kind of weird I love—the kind you get from talking to strangers! Not only did this man give me permission to eat a banana split (which I hadn't done since I was ten years old) but he also said something wise about celebrating the small victories in our lives.

Make a point of talking to a stranger this week.

Put your phone down in public spaces and notice who's around you. Make eye contact. Smile. It doesn't need to be artificial, just be willing to connect and see what happens.

Just an hour after writing this, I went to the grocery store to give it a try. There was a man standing next to me in the produce section, contemplating the green Romanesco over the regular white cauliflower. "The Romanesco is so pretty and fractal!" I exclaimed. "But I kind of prefer the regular old cauliflower."

"Exactly!" he replied. "My kids liked the purple cauliflower I got last time, but they didn't like it as much as the classic white." We went on to chat, and he shared that every time he comes to this produce market, he challenges himself to try something he's never tasted.

"Have you ever tried the Japanese sweet potatoes?" I pointed to the bin next to him.

"No!" he exclaimed.

I told him how my chef sweetie taught me how to bake them, slice them in disks, and fry them in coconut oil. We were both masked, but I could see the delight in his eyes. He elbow-bumped me and said, "Thank you for talking to me. People don't talk to each other anymore." And then he grabbed some sweet potatoes.

You might be shy or not quite know how to approach someone. Sometimes just offering a compliment is a great way in: "Ohhh . . . I love your curls!" Or "You have such great style!" You will know whether the person wants to continue chatting or you can leave it there.

We are meant to touch each other. We are social creatures, and we need each other to survive, both for our mental health and for the well-being of our communities. Even though I am writing this from a time of social distancing, where we are not allowed to embrace or get too close to our neighbors, this need feels so plain, so vital to our humanity. So though we have to remain socially distant, give talking to a stranger a try, sweet friends. See if it gives you a lift, a little burst of joy and aliveness. It is often the brightest spot in my day.

36. Host a Gratitude Party

YEARS AGO, an acquaintance of mine named Moe was going through serious medical issues with her eyes. She had a long journey of doctor's appointments, surgeries, and intense fear of losing her vision. She ultimately came through to the other side healthy, with her vision intact.

What she did to celebrate is something that says so much about her spirit: *she had a gratitude party!* She invited every single person who made her life easier at that time. She invited friends and family, but she also invited the dry cleaner, the nurses, the manicurist, the house cleaner, anyone who offered help, support, or kindness during a very vulnerable time in her life.

Everyone who arrived at the party knew they were connected by the same beautiful and profound thread—they had offered kindness and love to Moe! It has now become an annual tradition, a luncheon where Moe offers her heartfelt appreciation to these folks. Amazing, right?

Gratitude parties are a powerful way to raise your vibration, put more joy into the world, and allow people to feel more connected to you. In energetic terms, we can actually up-level our state of being from lower states like *fear*, *blame*, and *anger*, to higher states like *hopefulness*, *empowerment*, and *optimism*, by practicing gratitude. In other words, it will lift your spirits!

HERE'S HOW TO HOST A GRATITUDE PARTY:

1. Make a list of all of the people you love, who show you kindness, who make your life easier.
2. Invite them over for a Sunday brunch, a tea party, or a dinner. (Or, if that's not possible, have the party virtually!)
3. Make place cards for your guests that tell them what you appreciate about them. Be specific in how you acknowledge them.

Feeling introverted? Overwhelmed? In quarantine?

HERE ARE SOME OTHER WAYS TO DO IT:

- Have a gratitude party of one! Mark an evening (or morning) on your calendar and write handwritten notes thanking some special people in your life.
- If you're feeling more social, invite a few friends over to write thank-you notes with you! Play some music, light some candles, get some nice notecards, and have everyone write thank-you notes to people they appreciate. If you can't gather in person, you can write side by side on a video call.

However you do it, be specific. Tell your people *exactly* what you appreciate about them. Instead of a general "Thank you for being a good friend!" You might say, "Thank you for your open heart, for listening to me without judgment, and for letting me cry on your couch." Or, "Thank you for knowing exactly what I needed during my separation and for checking in via text each day to let me know you were there."

And here's some good news: You don't need to wait until you feel grateful to begin. You don't even need to be in a good mood! Appreciating others is a way we can invite gratitude to arise in us. . . . We don't need to wait until we are bubbling over with gratitude to extend it. We can extend it and then watch our hearts fill up with gratitude.

37. Amplify Someone's Joy

"DON'T YUCK MY YUM!"

I told my son this in the middle of our first Rummikub game. I had found an old set at a garage sale—the original kind from the seventies like my grandparents used to have. I still love how the tiles feel in my hands, kind of like mah-jongg tiles but with numbers on them instead. It's always been my favorite game.

"It's stupid. *Boring*," one of my children (who happened to not be winning at that point in the game) grumbled.

"Hey," I said, "this game is meaningful to me. I loved it as a kid. I was excited to share it with you. It actually hurts my feelings when you say you hate it."

"*I* like it!" the other one chimed in, trying to make the peace.

Maybe I shouldn't have taken it so personally. He was tired. He likes to win (who doesn't?). He's just a kid after all. But it's funny how when people rain on our parade (or as my kids learned in preschool, "yuck our yum"), it can hit us in an emotional place.

I used to have fantasies about parenthood where my kids enjoyed painting, cooking, and doing crafts with me. But alas, they would prefer to throw a football around, trade Pokémon cards, or play video games. Not being a fan of any of these things, I probably yuck their yum sometimes too.

It's natural that we want people to love what we love. Our joy is amplified when we share it with others. I think that's why it feels so personal when someone yucks our yum—it's like a rejection of some intimate part of ourselves.

But how would life be sweeter and richer if we got more curious?

Just recently, I learned how to throw a football the proper way. I had always dismissed football as totally boring and a game I have never really understood. But my kids happen to love it, and I see how happy they are when someone is willing to throw a ball with them. It's like throwing a ball to a puppy! And so I asked Nico to teach me. He carefully showed me where to put my fingers on the laces, how to grip the ball, and how to follow through with my arm even after the throw. When I managed to get a spiral, he would shout encouragingly, "That was great, Mom! You're getting better!"

Recently at the beach, I realized I was knee-deep in the ocean throwing a football over and over again to three boys in the water, who were competing to catch it. And I was having a great time. They dove after each throw, splashing in the water and having a blast. It was only when Nico said, "Nice spiral, Mom!" that I realized I had learned to throw a football and was totally enjoying myself. And the sweetness that my nine-year-old was my teacher made it all the better.

Today, the invitation is to consider some of the things we've closed ourselves off to. Maybe something our partner loves that we scoff at? *Karaoke, poker, jogging, that show on Netflix about desserts?* It could be anything, really.

What are some things your partner, kids, friends love that you've decided aren't for you?

The next time they ask you to play that game, watch that show, or just generally get excited about something, get interested! Get curious! Ask some questions. Notice if their eyes light up when they share. Yum their yum, people! Which is to say, amplify their joy by joining them in it.

38. Host a Storybowl

SEVERAL YEARS AGO, I HAD A VISION. I imagined a group of women (who didn't know each other) around a table, eating beautiful food, and passing around a bowl filled with story prompts. One by one, we would each tell an impromptu story about our lives.

This idea thrilled me for several reasons. The first is that I am bored at most parties. Small talk makes me tired. Witty banter makes my head hurt. I am the girl who will corner you at the party and go deep. You might be the only person I talk to that night, but we will be best buddies by the end of the evening.

Most importantly, I believe in the power of storytelling.

There is something really powerful that happens when humans circle up and tell stories. It is ancient and something we know in our bones. We are wired for this. And it is where so much learning and healing happens.

There is a quote from Mary Lou Kownacki (that Mr. Rogers loved) that pretty much sums it up: "There isn't anyone you couldn't love once you've heard their story."

I decided to call the game storybowl and imagined it would be one part creative gathering and one part healing circle. I started holding them regularly in the Bay Area, and they are pure joy. There is something really magical that unfolds when we are together. It's just the right mix of fun, connection, deep nourishment, compassion-building, and healing.

IT IS A WONDER TO DISCOVER HOW MANY GORGEOUS STORIES LIVE INSIDE EACH ONE OF US.

If the idea of holding a storybowl appeals to you, here are some steps to host your own.

1. Find a place to host it.
I am not a natural host. It makes me nervous, and I usually spend most of the night worrying if everyone is having a good time. For this reason, I host storybowls at other people's houses! Turns out a lot of my friends take great pleasure in hosting, so we are a good match.

You can also do this on a video-conferencing app! This eliminates the need to feed people and clean your house. Or if you are sheltered in place, you can host a safe storybowl!

2. Pick a date and time.
I have held both evening storybowls and storybowl brunches. They have both been really wonderful, so experiment and see what works best. Three hours is a great window of time to both eat and go around the circle twice. If you're on video, you might want to shorten the time frame.

3. Send out the invites.

It's great to gather a group of people who don't all know one another. Maybe you invite a few people and so does your host? This way there is a nice mix of new faces. I like to keep the circle to about five to eight people, including the hosts.

Here is a sample invitation (edit as you wish!):

Dear friend,

I'm excited to invite you to a creative gathering on *[enter date + time]*!

We will be eating a yummy meal and playing a game called storybowl, where we pass around a bowl of story prompts, and each person tells a spontaneous true story from their life based on the prompt they get.

Sounds like fun? Maybe a little scary?

Please know that this isn't about performing a great story. This is about a new way of sharing and connecting with each other. I promise it will be inspiring and delightful.

Would you like to join me? If you're a YES, just hit reply and say so! I will send you more details once I know who is coming.

With joy,
[Sign your name here]

4. Print these prompts or write your own.

The first time I hosted a storybowl, my friend and I scribbled story prompts down on ripped pieces of paper right before everyone arrived. It worked beautifully! We wrote things like: "a crime," "the worst gift," and "wise words." Since then, I have been honing in on which prompts work best and which fall a little flat.

On page 145 is a collection of prompts I have used over and over again. Feel free to use them or add your own! The trick is choosing themes that are open-ended and spark a memory. It's a way to find stories through the back door so even the storyteller is surprised by what they are sharing.

I recommend printing the prompts out on card stock so they feel more like cards and less like paper. Plus, they will last much longer!

5. Pick a bowl.
This is of course up to you. I chose a large, wide, wooden bowl that my brother-in-law made by hand. I like that the bowl is wide enough that you can swish the prompts around before you pick.

6. Open the circle.
When you're entering into sacred space, there is usually a ritual of some kind to open the circle. It might be called an icebreaker in more corporate settings . . . but in this context, it is a gentle way to get people to start sharing so that we can go deeper and create more intimacy later.

My favorite way to open the circle is to place a stack of angel cards into a bowl and have each person pick a card at random. (If you're not familiar with angel cards, they are a tiny deck of oracle cards that have one word written on each card: *vitality, joy, laughter, receptivity*, etc.)

As each person chooses a card, they share how that word resonates with something they are exploring in their life right now. Perhaps it serves as a theme or something they are working toward. Maybe it offers insight to what they are needing to call in. Whatever they want to share is perfect! (If you don't have angel cards, no problem. You can simply write words on small pieces of paper and make your own impromptu deck.)

7. The rules of the game:
Each storyteller gets two to three minutes to share. You can warn people that you will ring a bell if they need to wrap up their story soon. I always bring a vintage Fisher-Price Happy Apple chime toy. It looks very friendly, and the sound is light and pretty. Plus, it makes people laugh and invokes a sense of play.

Share the first thing that comes to mind when you read the prompt. Trust that whatever memory comes is the story that wants to be told. If you find yourself saying, "Oh no! I can't share that," that's the story that we want to hear. If you tell yourself, "That's not an interesting enough story," that's the one we want to hear!

This is not a performance. We are not trying to tell the best story in the room. This is a sharing practice, a place to connect, an opportunity to allow others to see us.

No cross talk, please. Although oohs and aahs and other signs of engagement are welcome! Just honor that the person telling the story has the floor. We want to all be the most generous listeners we can be.

Sometimes a prompt falls flat. You watch the person's face wrinkle in confusion as they search their mind for something story-worthy. Finally they declare, "I got nothin'." In this case, you can encourage the player to pass their prompt to someone else or place it back in the bowl and take another.

When things go deep, this is a good thing. This means that you are holding space in such a way that the group feels safe to let their real selves out. There are sometimes tears at storybowl. Welcome whatever shows up and know that your job is to simply stay present. Together we can hold big feelings.

Don't forget to close the circle after the last person shares a story.
1. Go around the circle and have each person share what the experience was like for them. This gives people a chance to debrief and put words to their experience—one that might have been more profound than you realized.
2. Go around and have each person share one word that describes how they feel now (e.g., *connected*, *full-hearted*, *open*, *joyful*). This is a simple (and quick!) way to acknowledge what impact the storybowl had on them without going into too much explanation.
3. Offer a heartfelt thank-you to everyone for showing up and sharing with the group. Acknowledge the courage it takes to show up and be seen and how honored you were to catch their stories.

If all that sounds like way too much, simply cut out your favorite prompts and put them in a bowl (or a jar) to use with your family as conversation starters. My kids and I love to do this at the dinner table!

AN ANIMAL ENCOUNTER	HOW WE MET	GHOST STORY	A SCANDAL
THE WISEST WORDS	THE WORST GIFT	A STORY OF SERENDIPITY	THE WORST JOB
A PLACE YOU USED TO LOVE TO GO	SOMETHING YOU LOST	SOMETHING YOU FOUND	YOUR SUPERPOWER
A FOOD STORY	A LOVE STORY	WORST PARTY EVER	A TIME WHEN YOU SHOULD HAVE SAID NO
A TIME WHEN YOU SHOULD HAVE SAID YES	SOMETHING YOU USED TO KNOW HOW TO DO	MEETING MY HERO	BETWEEN WORLDS
A STORY ABOUT A NAME (YOURS OR SOMEONE ELSE'S)	CELEBRITY SIGHTING	SOMETHING YOU REALLY WANTED AND FINALLY GOT	A TIME WHEN YOU SURPRISED YOURSELF
A FIRST	A STORY OF MISCHIEF	A BAD TRIP	A TIME YOU GOT INTO TROUBLE
A SUPERNATURAL EXPERIENCE	SOMETHING YOU USED TO BELIEVE	A BLESSING IN DISGUISE	A FIRST KISS
THE KINDEST THING ANYONE HAS EVER DONE FOR YOU	A MOMENT OF WONDER	A TIME WHEN YOU GOT CAUGHT	A STRANGER

SUCCESS OR FAILURE:
THE TRUTH OF A LIFE
REALLY HAS LITTLE TO
DO WITH ITS QUALITY.
THE QUALITY OF LIFE
IS IN PROPORTION,
ALWAYS, TO THE
CAPACITY FOR DELIGHT.
THE CAPACITY FOR
DELIGHT IS THE GIFT OF
paying attention.

—JULIA CAMERON

CHAPTER 6

CREATING WONDER FOR

Others

BACK IN 2005, my then husband, Matt—who had a lot of wild, creative ideas—said, "Guess what? We're going to build a public park in a parking space in the middle of downtown San Francisco! Will you take photos?" I thought he was crazy, or would be arrested, or both.

"Wait, *what* are you doing?" I asked.

"Okay, so have you ever noticed that there is very little public green space in downtown SF? My artist friends and I are going to build a park in a parking space to highlight this! We looked up the city code, and the law doesn't explicitly say that you have to have a vehicle in a parking space, so as long as you are paying the meter, you can ostensibly do whatever you want within that space. You're essentially leasing the space from the city for a couple of hours!" He looked excited, even gleeful about this loophole.

I was nervous but agreed to be the photographer for this wild little guerrilla art project.

The following week, Matt and his collaborators at Rebar (their art collective) chose a parking space in a busy part of downtown San Francisco. They rolled out grass sod, placed a park bench, put a big potted tree down, and made a sign that read: "Pay the meter to keep the park open!"

We put a stack of quarters in and then watched from across the street to see what would happen. To our delight, people started interacting with the park. Random people sat on the bench to have lunch, passersby took off their shoes to feel the grass between their toes, business people were smiling and putting their coins in. Within minutes it was functioning as a tiny public park! People loved it. Rebar called their project Park(ing), which eventually became Park(ing) Day.

The next day, I posted this image (see previous page) on my blog, and it started to get passed around the internet. When a huge website got hold of it, it went viral, and the mayor's office called. I was sure this was when Matt was going to get arrested! But it turns out that the mayor at the time, Gavin Newsom, called because he loved it as well! And several big non-profits in San Francisco wanted to partner with Rebar to host more Park(ing) Day interventions.

I think what made this project so magnetic is that it was the most delightful kind of activism. Rebar was commenting on the lack of public green space in downtown San Francisco (how the city's urban design privileged cars over humans), but they managed to communicate this in a way that was so full of delight that everyone wanted to be part of it. It became a celebration of creativity and posed a joyful possibility for our city.

Park(ing) Day turned into a global event where every year (on the third Friday in September in cities all over the globe), parking spaces are transformed into temporary public parks. People have created all sorts of wonderful things in parking spaces—bicycle repair stations, a free lemonade stand, a lawn-bowling course, a public kiddie pool—all in the spirit of offering something delightful to their community.

These Park(ing) Day events resulted in the very first parklets being created in San Francisco (and then in other cities), which are more permanent takeovers of parking spaces and are specifically designed to be public open spaces (pocket parks) for people to relax in.

This was only the first of many incredible projects that Rebar dreamed up. They created all sorts of wonder-filled experiences that invited people to ask questions about how their cities were designed and invited regular people to be agents in creating them.

Most resonant for me is that they created experiences of wonder for others. They went off-script and created surprise and magic. They reimagined ordinary life so that it woke us up to new ideas about how things could be.

This chapter is about creating wonder for others. This could be as simple as sending something artful in the mail or as elaborate as hosting a neighborhood water balloon fight on a hot day. It could be planting love notes in books at the library so that one day in the future, someone will find them and they will feel like notes from the divine. It could be telling everyone to blow bubbles at the park at exactly the same moment, or setting up lawn chairs in your yard with a sign that reads, "I'm not busy. Come chat with me."

Wonder wakes us up. It allows for new possibilities and dreams. It reminds us that we have the power to create the story of our lives. That we can fill it with color and magic.

And guess what? You don't have to wait. I'm going to show you how. On the following pages you will find a variety of projects that are invitations to create wonder and delight for others. They are designed to be accessible enough that anyone can do them—whether you consider yourself an artist or not. Start out by committing to do just one of the projects at first.

I want you to have the experience of being a Wonder Maker. It is truly the most joyful job in the world.

39. Make a Wish Tree

SEVERAL YEARS AGO (inspired by a wish tree project Yoko Ono started in 1981), my boys and I made our very own wish tree in front of our house. It was a playful thing—something I had always wanted to do, simply for the delight of making something with my hands and bringing something fun to my community.

Little did I know it would be the very best thing I did all year.

Little did I know it would be a source of daily joy.

Little did I know that the local middle school students would stop by and hang their wishes on the tree.

Little did I know that reading these pieces of paper would open my heart and allow me to feel the sweetest kind of connection.

Whenever we meet a new neighbor these days and they ask where we live, we proudly say, "Over there by the wish tree!"

And they always get excited.

Recently, when we met a new family, their eyes got wide. "That's yours? The wish tree was the first thing we saw when we moved to the neighborhood! It made us feel like we were home."

Wanna know something kinda fun and poetic? The tree that all the wishes hang from is a lemon tree. It's beautiful, but the lemons are inedible—sour, bitter, and lumpy. I love the poetry of this: The bitter lemon tree that has been fashioned into a wish tree. The bitter tree that is bringing people hope and delight and a moment of reflection and connection.

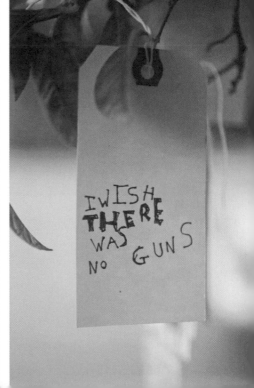

Here's how we did it:

1. Get some shipping tags from the office supply store. I recommend getting the ones that already have the string attached so people can use those to tie the tag to the tree themselves.
2. Make a sign that reads, "Make a wish!" You can use anything sturdy, like a thick poster board or a canvas. It will get a bit tattered in the weather as time goes on, but that's okay. You could also hang up a clipboard like my friend Nicole did on her tree in Portland, Oregon.
3. The shipping tags we purchased came in a plastic box that we duct-taped to the tree. This way, the tags were shielded from rain and we could put markers right inside the plastic box. If you don't find tags with a plastic box, you can fashion your own. You will just need a vessel that will keep the tags and markers dry.
4. Make a few wishes yourself to get the magic started!

The other day I saw a teenage boy carrying a skateboard walk up to my door. He left something on the stoop, and I grumbled, "I'm sick of those pizza joints leaving their menus on my steps!" I ran out to see what he left and my heart melted:

Can you please
Put out more wishing
tree tags!!!
                    thank you :)

40. Leave a Love Note in a Public Place

WHEN MY COLLEAGUE JEN LEMEN AND I WERE SPEAKERS at a conference several years ago in Portland, Oregon, we did something a little crazy. The subject of our talk was Mondo Beyondo (a course we taught about mani-festing big dreams) and we wanted to offer the participants something that felt outrageously kind. We ended up handwriting five hundred love notes on index cards that we then taped underneath each seat in the theater before we were due onstage. We took this job seriously, lounging on the couches at the Ace Hotel with Sharpies in hand, channeling each note with every cell of our being: *What might this person need to hear?* And we'd see what message would come to us in that moment.

Turns out it takes a long time to write this many notes! And throughout the weekend you could find us snuggled up on our hotel room beds, on park benches across from the museum, and at bars drinking cocktails late at night writing, writing. . . .

"Do we really have to do all of these?" I would ask Jen when I was losing steam.

"YES!" she would say emphatically.

On Sunday, at the end of our talk, we asked everyone to look under their chair for a special note written just for them. There were shouts of joy and surprise and more than a few tears . . . then they all rose to their feet and cheered. We felt like rock stars of love and kindness! And deeply connected to every single person in the room.

Years later, I saw a Facebook thread from an attendee asking folks if they still had their love note from that first conference. I watched as a steady stream of people shared photos of their index cards—pasted inside their journals, attached to their refrigerators, on their altars. I was astounded and moved. These notes were so simple, but they felt like magic to the recipients. (And they kept them!) With all the beautiful intentions we put into them, they were received as the transmissions of love and encouragement we had intended.

LOVE NOTES FOR YOU

On the following page is a set of love notes that you can cut out for your own personal love-bombing escapades! Or, if you're not keen on cutting them out, you can copy them down on index cards (or Post-it notes) and love-bomb away!

Here are some ideas for places to leave them:
- In public restrooms.
- Inside books at the library.
- In the crook of a tree.
- At the farmers market in the apple bin.
- On bicycles or cars that are parked on the street.
- In the jacket pocket of a loved one.

Or . . .

You can create a little bowl of love notes just for you! I like to close my eyes and choose one at random whenever I need a little inspiration.

You are lovable.

You can trust your intuition.

It's not too late for you.

Support is all around you.

Let it be simple.

The answer is yes.

What makes you come alive?

This is not the end of the story.

You can begin again.

You have everything you need to begin.

What tiny, brave step could you take today?

Everything is going to be okay.

Your longings are divine, listen closely.

It's okay to ask for what you want.

The world needs your gifts.

What if there's nothing to fix about you?

Don't wait for a better day.

We are all rooting for you.

Write your own

41. Balloon Poetry

THE FIRST TIME I SAW poet Amy Turn Sharp and blogger Jordan Ferney's balloon-poetry collaborations on Instagram, I was filled with an *Oh my God, why didn't I think of that?* kind of glee. They hung gorgeous little phrases on urban walls with gold-letter balloons. I was so inspired by this series, I immediately wanted to do my own!

The first question was: *What do I want to say? And therefore, which letters do I purchase?* As I write this in 2020, we are mid-pandemic and most of the country is still sheltered in place. I wondered what words would feel like a little love letter, something uplifting for the community to see.

I CONSIDERED:

- *You are loved.*
- *The light in you is contagious.*
- *Joy is on its way.*
- *Love always wins.*
- *You are a wonder.*

I settled on *Remember your magic . . .* Short and sweet. Up for interpretation. A reminder that we all have magic inside us, the kind that allows for the unexpected, the miraculous, the joyful. Once the balloons arrived (they come with instructions and a special straw you can use to blow them up), I just needed to inflate them and choose a background.

I didn't want to vandalize any walls (and I liked the idea of having the sign in my own neighborhood), so I asked a neighbor to use their fence that faced out onto a well-trafficked street. I got my son to help me hang it up with ribbon, and we used thumbtacks to secure it to the fence. Easy peasy! And since it's close to my house, I can keep an eye on it and take it down if it deflates or falls down.

As a life coach, I often ask people: "If you had access to a billboard and could tell the world anything, what would it be?" Their response says something important about what they value in life and who they are at their core. Clients say things like "Just be you," or "Be kind to yourself," or "Don't postpone joy." If you're stuck on what to say, I offer this question as a little springboard.

Ready to try? Here's how to do it.
1. Decide on what you want to say.
2. Order those particular balloon letters or purchase them at your local party store.
3. Blow them up, string them together (the balloons should come with some ribbon, and there are loops at the top of the balloons for threading).
4. Tack them up in your neighborhood or somewhere in need of an uplifting message. If you're worried about vandalizing, perhaps you can set them up on your garage door or somewhere on your property.
5. Share the photos with me! Use the hashtags #wonderseeker and #balloonpoetry.

42. Create Some Mail Art

WAY BACK IN THE NINETIES, I was *realllly* into mail art. There was an entire subculture of us making quirky, often postcard-size pieces of collage art and sending them through the mail to one lucky recipient. These pieces were never published, nor were they widely seen (this is pre-internet). It was usually just artist to artist, made for the pure delight of the exchange of creativity and love of the process. I know people who still send mail art today!

For me, mail art looked like me spending hours every night with glue sticks and scissors in hand, cutting up magazines and creating tiny works of art. I even came up with my own mail-art name—*Sparkle Pudding*—and would sign my work that way. Of course, it was equally fun to receive things in the mail—zines and teeny-tiny books made by hand, weird postcards with the lyrics to songs written all over them, or an entire story written on the tiniest possible sheet of paper and tucked into a matchbox.

One of my signature moves was to incorporate photo booth pictures—the vintage kind with real film images—into my art. There was a photo booth near my house that happened to have a trunk full of wigs and other props you could use to make your photos more playful. My friends and I claimed it as our unofficial mini theater. Oh the time before smartphone selfies!

When I was courting my now ex-husband, Matt, I decided to do something romantic. One day, I had painted a portrait of a woman on a large piece of card stock but wasn't super excited about it when it was done. As I contemplated throwing it in the garbage, I had a better idea. What if I created a giant mail-art project? I drew a grid on top of it and started cutting the painting up into postcard-size pieces. Pretty soon I had a stack of abstract painted postcards that were colorful and cool and even more interesting than the original piece. Each day I sent him a postcard in the mail. I left the painting as it was, but on the other side I wrote him something loving, transcribed an inspiring quote, or just wrote a quick note (along with his name and address of course).

Day by day, he received each of these postcards in the mail. After about a week, he started to notice something—they were fitting together like puzzle pieces! By the time he had received all the postcards, he had put together the original painting. (This is arguably the best gift I ever gave him.)

Why am I telling you all of this? I want to inspire you to create some postal art yourself, of course. Now, more than ever, getting something friendly in the mail is a wonderful surprise! If we were all in the same room, I would suggest a postcard party where we dump a bunch of watercolors, markers, glue sticks, and magazines on the table and go to town. But maybe we can just imagine that we are all doing this together. Or you can host some friends to do this with you on video or in person.

SOME SUGGESTIONS:

1. Cut up some watercolor paper (on the heavier side) or card stock in the dimensions of a standard postcard. Or repurpose your postcard-size junk mail (like those reminders from the dentist) and collage over the front.
2. Order or buy some really cute stamps at the post office.
3. Start decorating! Paint those puppies. Write a quote in cursive across it with a nice pen. Collage something fun and colorful across the front. Do a bunch of them at a time.
4. Think of people you appreciate and decide to delight them today.
5. This process is *very forgiving*. You don't need to fancy yourself an artist to totally rock this project. If you get stuck, just write: I ADORE YOU or YOU ARE AMAZING! in your very best handwriting, and you will make this person's day. Guaranteed.

Not sure who to write to? You could send mail to nursing homes where folks might be lonely, make some artsy get-out-the-vote postcards if there's an election coming up, or leave something nice for your mail carrier.

43. Install a Fairy Door

THIS IS A FAIRY DOOR. There's a similar door left by fairies in Golden Gate Park in San Francisco—a door with little baubles inside—and word was getting around fast about this magical portal in the park. It seemed everyone wanted to find it!

I had been searching for it for months, unsuccessfully, when a friend told me a hilarious story.

"I was changing Owen's diaper in a little woodsy area near the Japanese Tea Garden. You know, for privacy, right? When suddenly I looked up and I was surrounded by a team of Segways. They were all looking for a fairy door precisely in the grove where I had stopped! It was disturbing and surreal!"

She gave me the best instructions she could. *Along the side of the Japanese Tea Garden, there is a fence, a path, a log, etc. . . .* but I was still confused when I went searching for it again the next time. Recently, I had a date with my friend Danny who had flown in for a David Hockney show at the de Young Museum in San Francisco. After marveling at the paintings for hours, I proposed we get some air and search for the mythical fairy door, rumored to be nearby. Whenever Danny came to visit from NYC, I always made a point of taking him somewhere quirky and unusual. Once, it was to get a chakra healing at the Psychic Eye Book Shops; another time it was to see the Musée Mécanique—an interactive museum full of vintage penny-arcade games. When I realized we were close to the Japanese Tea Garden, it seemed like the perfect thing.

We asked around and eventually found it! Inside were wishes and bells, rocks and shells, love notes and acorns. In the end, it wasn't the door itself that was so spectacular. Why were so many people searching for it then? People are hungry for a sense of enchantment. They are longing to experience something that feels magical.

And guess what? You don't need to search. You can make your own! You can create your very own world for others to discover. You can be the Wonder Maker who inspires a sense of magic in others.

Here's how to install your own fairy door:
1. **Buy a little door at a craft store.** This doesn't need to be an official fairy door—it can be as simple as a dollhouse door resting against a tree.
2. **Find a tree that looks like a suitable gathering place for fairies.** The fairy door on page 169 is located right in front of our house. You could also find one out in nature or in an urban place that would inspire the imagination of people who stumble upon it.
3. **Install the fairy door.** We didn't even need to attach the door to the tree. We just nestled it in the dirt and it seemed pretty secure. The neighbor girls from downstairs surprised me by taking it several steps further. They made an entryway with tiny rocks, placed fresh flowers, mushrooms, and even created a place for the fairies to keep their firewood.

It brings me joy every time I see it. And hopefully, it brightens the days of passersby as well.

THE OBJECT
ISN'T TO MAKE ART,
IT'S TO BE IN THAT
WONDERFUL STATE
WHICH MAKES ART
inevitable.

–ROBERT HENRI, *THE ART SPIRIT*

44. Go Off-Script

WHAT MAKES FOR EXPERIENCES THAT ARE MORE MAGICAL than the everyday? What are the essential ingredients that make something truly memorable? And how can we architect for peak moments in our lives and in the lives of others?

Bestselling authors of *The Power of Moments* and *Made to Stick*, Chip and Dan Heath argue that "anything that breaks the script causes a little jolt of surprise, and surprise is what makes things memorable."

Memorable, you say?

I think of my high school boyfriend Albie, who hired an ice-cream man to take us to the prom. I thought we'd be getting a ride from someone's parents, but when I heard strange music outside, my girlfriend and I ran to the window. Our dates were outside next to the ice-cream truck.

"Your chariot awaits!" they shouted up.

We climbed over freezers full of ice-cream sandwiches and Popsicles, sitting on each other's laps since there was not much room, but we didn't care. We were living inside the most wonderful story.

I think of the time I was crushing on the barista at the café I got my bagel and coffee from every morning. One day, I ordered my usual but added a plain bagel to go. In a quiet corner of the restaurant, I pulled a black Sharpie out of my bag and wrote my name on one side of the bagel and my phone

number on the other. Then I tucked it into a paper bag and handed it to him. "This one is for you," I said, blushing wildly. Then I hightailed it out of the store! He called that very day.

I think of my friends Chris and Jacques, who surprised me on my thirty-ninth birthday. I hadn't planned on celebrating, since I had just given birth to my second son a few days before and was still recovering and moving slowly. The doorbell rang, and I saw two figures, both with boxes covering their faces. The boxes were wrapped like presents, and I heard a muffled, "Open up your gifts!" As I lifted off the tops of the boxes, I shrieked when I saw their faces underneath. I was beyond surprised and elated. It would have been enough that they had flown all the way from Hana, Maui, to surprise me, but the fact that they dressed like presents made the whole thing truly magical.

Chris and Jacques are masters of going off-script. This is likely why I have so many delicious memories of them. They are the ones who will pick up a bag of rose petals at the florist on the way to get you at the airport and throw them in the air as soon as they see you. They will drag you out of bed at 4:00 a.m. to drive to see the sunrise somewhere beautiful. They will invite you to visit and within hours of arrival, you will be in a poodle costume in the middle of a summer solstice parade learning a dance routine with ten other poodles.

The first time I visited Chris at his new place in Santa Barbara, he instructed me to take off my watch. "They aren't allowed at La Cabaña," he told me. (What he whimsically called the property he was renting a little house on, with acres of lemon and avocado orchards.) When we arrived, he placed a genie hat on my head and handed me a large glass bottle. Then he led me out to the backyard, where there was a magic carpet—an oriental rug suspended from a tree. He photographed me, erased the ropes in Photoshop, and voilà! There I was on a flying carpet.

More recently, after being engaged for fourteen years, Chris planned a surprise wedding for Jacques. All seventy-five of us kept the big secret for months! The greatest pleasure was witnessing the utter glee on Chris's face. . . . To pull off such an elaborate surprise and to have it so gracefully received was the most amazing thing to witness.

Not everyone lives as colorfully as these two, but we can learn something from them. To me, going off-script just means that we are taking something ordinary, something that we would usually do—*drive the kids to school*; *make dinner at home*; *go pick up a friend at the airport*—and making it as memorable as possible.

- For example, when you're at the grocery store and the flowers catch your eye, ask yourself if there is anyone in your life who would really love them. Then hop over to their house and leave them at their door.

- When you pick up the kids from school, maybe you say, "Hey, let's go see a movie and have popcorn for dinner!" instead of the usual head-home-have-dinner routine.

- Or maybe, instead of the standard *Hey, it's me, call me back* voice mail, you leave that person a voice message with a list of things you love most about them.

I like this notion of breaking the script because it speaks to the element of wonder that is about surprise, about the unexpected. I love that we can intentionally infuse a bit of magic into our lives (and in the lives of others) and create a moment we'll remember for a long time.

Your challenge this week: have an off-script adventure.
(Something small. No surprise weddings required!)

45. Host a Bubble Flash Mob

HAVE YOU EVER WANTED TO BE PART OF A FLASH MOB? You know those spontaneous dance routines that spring up at shopping malls out of nowhere? From people who look like ordinary shoppers? Being part of one of those is definitely on my Wonder List. But there is another type of flash mob you should know about too—one that is even more accessible and easy to pull off—the bubble flash mob!

I teamed up with my friends, author Sherry Richert Belul and Ian Fratar (who have done several of these at Dolores Park in San Francisco), for the most delicious day of creative magic!

Here's how to do it:
- Get a big box of those party-favor-size bubble containers.
- Go to a crowded park on a beautiful day and start handing them out to everyone you see! People are delighted to get something for free, and who doesn't love bubbles?
- Tell them, "Start blowing these bubbles at exactly 11:11 a.m. Not a moment before!" (We usually start handing them out about ten minutes prior to launch. This way, it's fresh on their minds and they won't forget.) These people become your coconspirators!

And that's it! At exactly 11:11 a.m. (or whatever time you declare), everyone across the entire park starts blowing their bubbles at the same time! It is *pure magic*. And everyone feels like a part of it. Even the people who arrived later, who didn't get any bubbles, get to have a moment of pure wonder that you have gifted them!

sar·cas·ti·cal·ly (sär-kas′ti-k'l-i, sär-ka...) ... in a sarcastic manner.

sar·ce·net (särs′net), n. [Anglo-Fr. sarzin... M.E. Sarsin, Sarasene, Saracen], a soft silk... for ribbons, linings, etc.

sar·co- (sär′kō, sär′kə), [< Gr. sarx, sarkos... combining form meaning flesh, as in sarcolo... before a vowel, sarc-.

sar·co·carp (sär′kə-kärp′), n. [sarco- + -carp], in... 1. the fleshy part of a stone fruit, as in the plu... loosely, any fleshy fruit.

sar·col·o·gy (sär-kol′ə-ji), n. [sarco- + -logy], the br... of anatomy that deals with the soft tissues of the b...

sar·co·ma (sär-kō′mə), n. [pl. SARCOMAS (-...) COMATA (-mə-tə)], [Mod. L.; Gr. sarkōma (...) any of various malignant tumors that... nective tissue, or in tissue developed from the conn... blast and not epithelial; cf. carcinoma...

sar·co·ma·toid (sär-kō′mə-toid′), adj. ... comas through the nature of a ...

sar·co·ma·to·sis (sär-kō′mə-tō′sis), n. a condition... acterized by a more or less general...

sar·co·ma·tous (sär-kō′mə-təs), adj. ... or having the nature of a ...

sar·coph·a·gus (sär-kof′ə-gəs), n. ... SARCOPHAGI (...) sarkos, flesh + ... limestone ... among the ...

CHAPTER 7

EVERYDAY Magic

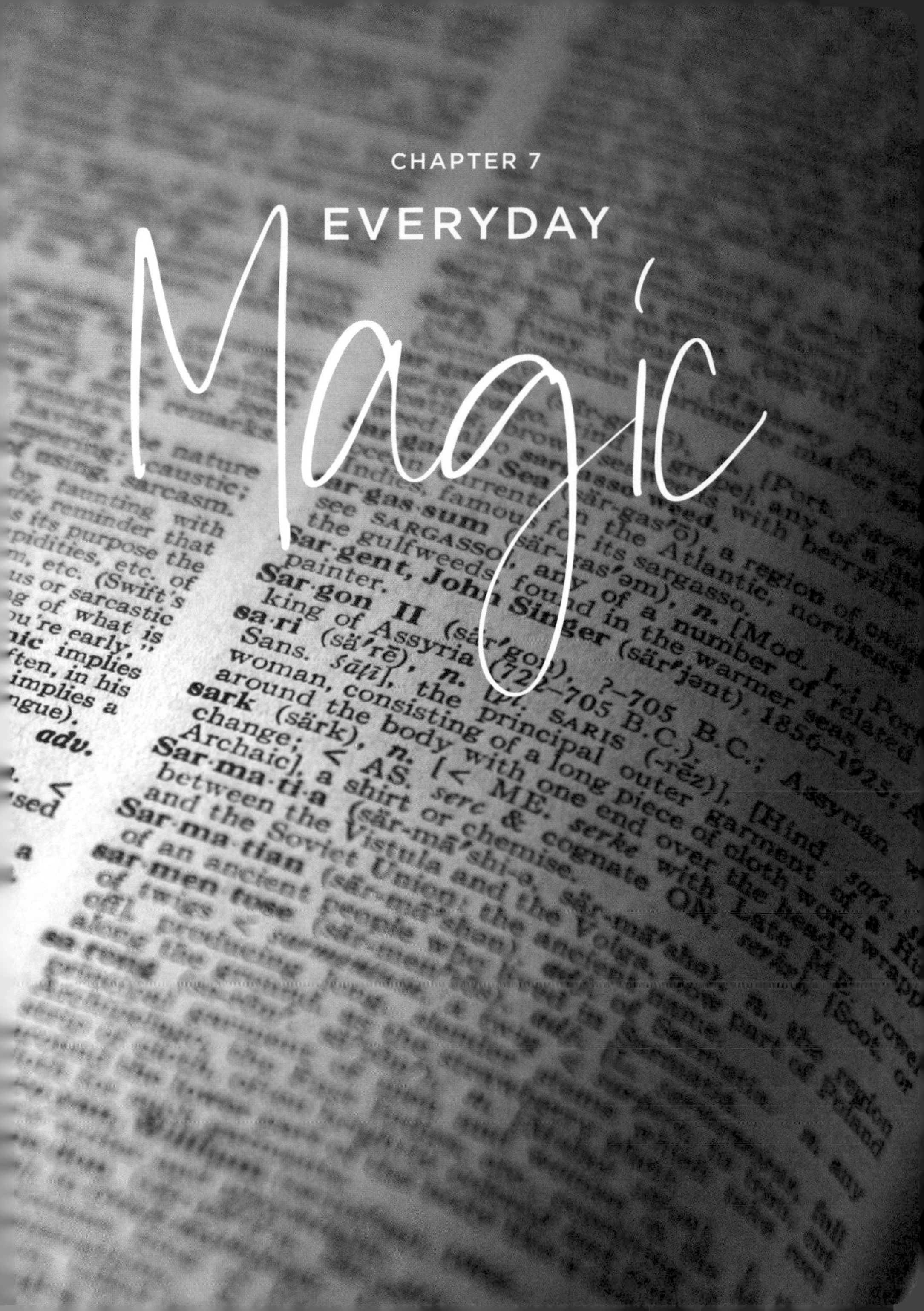

WHEN I FIRST ENCOUNTERED THE AUTHOR AND ARTIST SARK'S WORK, it was a revelation—*Wait, books can look like this?* They were creative and colorful—endlessly inspiring and positive—printed in her whimsical hand-writing, and looked more like personal journals than traditional books. I was simultaneously inspired and full of envy. *My books have already been written!* I thought. This of course wasn't true (I was just feeling a deep resonance), but as I would learn from SARK later, "Jealousy is a map, it shows us where we want to go." It was clear that these books were bread crumbs, leading me toward where I was going in my own creative life.

My path wasn't always clear to me. I had been a creative kid, choreographing dance routines in the driveway, painting rocks and selling them door-to-door, and making jewelry from tiny seed beads. But once I landed in high school, I had largely abandoned my creative pursuits in favor of cheerleading, boys, and my studies. My family urged me to do something practical, and since I was good at math, I ended up getting a degree in business economics from UC Santa Barbara. I got good grades but knew the whole way through that it wasn't my heart's calling.

Right after college, I moved to New Orleans to help my parents open a business there. One day, while strolling through the French Quarter, I stumbled upon the Bottom of the Cup Tea Room. It was one of those metaphysical shops with books, candles, incense, and crystals. In the back of the store (in private booths with curtains drawn), they gave tarot and palm readings. A silver-haired woman smiled at me from one of the booths.

"Would you like a reading?" she asked.

She shuffled an oversize deck of cards several times before laying out three piles in front of me. "Middle, left, or right?" she asked.

"Left," I replied.

"Okay." She nodded and moved the other piles to the side. Then she laid the cards out in a pattern in front of us.

"You're an artist," she began.

I was delighted by this. I had gotten so far away from this in school and was just finding my way back to painting. For her to say this was a powerful affirmation (and a kind of permission slip) for me to pursue the path that was calling to me.

But then she went on. "But your real work is as a healer. You will heal people through your art."

All of the hairs on my arms pricked up. All I could think was: *Yes! Yes! But how?*

As I rediscovered my artist's heart, I also discovered mail art. This was a subculture of people who, like myself, loved the medium of making art specifically for the mail. We'd collage postcards, make tiny books, cut and paste remnants of everyday life. Think ticket stubs, feathers, drops of red wine, repurposed matchbooks, and cocktail umbrellas. We made these things not for the market or for a readership, but for *one person only*—the one who would receive this treasure in their mailbox. It was a gift. Pure and simple. A creative way to communicate between old friends who lived across miles. (Learn how to make your own mail art on page 166.)

There was one particular house I lived in during my next, shorter stay in Santa Barbara, where all of us roommates spent nearly every night on the floor of our bungalow with scissors and glue, photo booth pictures and glitter, drinking wine, listening to music, and making things. The mailman knew we always got the best mail!

A DESIGNER IN TRAINING

From the outside, all this cutting and pasting wasn't amounting to much. I had decided to move to San Francisco from Santa Barbara, was working at a clothing store, and was painting and collaging in my spare time. I was having lots of fun but feeling aimless. What I didn't know is that I was also training myself for a step on my future path.

One night, I told a friend how I would sometimes ask the dictionary questions—point to a word at random and get some clarity and insight.

Her eyes got big. "Really? Let's try it now!"

I closed my eyes and moved my fingers along the side of the book. "Give me a word for something I should be aware of that I'm not aware of."

Then I opened the dictionary and slid my finger down the page. I opened my eyes and saw the word my finger had landed on: it was *sark*.

My friend was confused. "What's a *sark*?"

"It means a chemise or a shirt . . . ," I read slowly. "But it's also the name of an author I've always admired." At this point, I found a SARK book and opened it to show her. The page I opened to read: "If your work isn't your dream or leading to your dream, quit sooner rather than later."

"Oh my God," I said to my friend, goose bumps all over my body. "I'm going to quit my job and work for SARK."

I decided I would connect with her energetically by making her something. That something turned into an accordion book full of photographs and quotes, boa feathers and paint, and a letter introducing myself. Because I only had her publisher's address, I didn't think it would ever reach her, but I felt moved to connect with her just the same.

Several weeks later, I got a call from SARK's office. Not only did the little book reach her, but they called to tell me that *they couldn't wait to meet me*. To meet *me*! Apparently that little book functioned as an accidental portfolio piece and I had intrigued them.

The day we met felt less like a job interview and more like a reunion of old friends.

"I love your face!" was the first thing SARK said as she beamed at me.

I remember being so moved when she showed me their company's mission statement, which was about using creativity to uplift and inspire others. It spoke not only to the artist in me, but to the healer in me too, the part that wanted my creative life to serve others. It was the beginning of a brand-new life, one that aligned with my spirit. In a world where I had no idea what was next for me, where my only professional experience was selling coffee or clothes, I was floored to have suddenly found a dream job.

And my first assignment there? It was to create a line of licensed gift products based on SARK's art. I literally sat on the rug and cut and pasted SARK quotes and artwork into greeting cards and stationery. Turns out all those hours of mail art were the perfect training for a future of design and artmaking in the real world. I had exactly what I needed for this next step on my path.

I love this story because it affirms something I believe wholeheartedly—that whatever you are curious about, whatever delights you and brings you joy is precisely what will take you on the path toward your deepest dreams. You don't need to connect the dots or even understand it. In fact, it might be better if you don't. Just do it for the joy of it.

And know that nothing, *absolutely nothing*, you've ever done is wasted.

This chapter is about everyday magic—the kind where serendipity finds us, wishes come true, miracles happen, and there is a beautiful call-and-response with the Universe. I don't pretend to know all of what this dance entails, but I do have some stories I'm excited to share with you. And I do know this: your delight is taking you somewhere. I'm going to teach you how to follow your delight.

46. Set an Intention

ONE CHRISTMAS DAY, soon after my divorce, I woke up alone. My ex-husband and I co-parent our two boys, and since I'm Jewish, they usually stay with their dad for this holiday. But still, there was that feeling, that ache in my chest of *Where are my children? How is it that I don't get to see their sweet faces beaming and bursting as they open presents today?* I imagined them tearing at the paper with glee, squealing as they removed each treasure from their stocking. I imagined them with their grandparents and cousins getting so much delicious attention, playing board games in their pajamas, eating pancakes.

We have these moments, right? Those times when we take a mental inventory and judge how far we've come. *How the heck did I get here? I never thought my life would look like this. What have I accomplished? How is it possible that I'm a single mom? This is so strange and not at all what I planned. . . .*

As I was beginning to get a bit blue, I looked down at my phone. *Want to come downstairs and watch the girls open presents?* It was my sweet neighbor in the apartment downstairs, a fellow single mama with two little girls. She gets it. She is the one who, when I am away on a trip and flying home, will turn on some lights in my apartment and put the heater on so that I don't come home to a cold, empty house. That kind of friend.

Yes! I texted back, smiling.

I came down and watched them open gifts. They cheered after every package was opened. I took in their pure delight—the perfect proxy—and it was so good. And the girls had made me gifts as well, a friendship bracelet in oranges and purples and a gorgeous hand-knit square in ombré blues, perfect for my altar.

Knowing how hard this day can be, I had started a tradition the year before of hiking just north of San Francisco in Tennessee Valley. It's a long, gorgeous walk to the ocean. You land at a wild little cove with roiling waves, not the kind of water you would dare swim in, but the kind you *bow* to. The power and beauty is massive and overwhelming. You feel small there, but in the best possible way. You feel held because it's so clear that it's not about you, that there is so much more, that there is an entire Universe that has big plans. I like being humbled this way. It was the perfect place to take my tender little heart.

I picked up a smooth, black stone and held it in my palm, facing the water. *May I let go of whatever stands in the way of love and joy.* I chanted this to myself as I took a few steps toward the water. *May I let go of whatever stands in the way of love and joy!* Then I threw the rock and watched the waves swallow it up.

As I set this intention and watched the rock disappear, it reminded me of those pneumatic tubes from back in the day. Remember when our parents would go through the drive-through at the bank, deposit a check into the tube, and it would shoot straight up into the ether? I couldn't figure out where exactly it went, but I like to imagine it went up to the sky, to the clouds, to the world of magical things!

This is also how I like to imagine our dreams, our wishes, and our intentions . . . like the one I made at the ocean. We write it, speak it, and then we let it go. We put it in the cosmic pneumatic tube and it shoots up into the unknown.

I know that setting intentions is powerful. So I invite you to set one now!

- What would you like to call into your life?
- How would you like to feel?
- What are you hungry for?

You can use this book as a way to call in more everyday magic.

It will help wake up your creativity and your aliveness. It will open your heart and help you find your self-compassion. It will remind you that wishes come true, miracles happen, and there is a beautiful call-and-response with the Universe. Start with a simple intention and see what unfolds.

47. Refuse to Know Anything for 24 Hours

"BUT PONIES AREN'T REAL . . . ," my son Nico said to me as we walked away from his kindergarten class, his warm little palm in mine.

I laughed, "Yes they are! They are small horses!"

"Oh, right!" he replied. "It's donkeys that aren't real!"

And for a moment I didn't know what was real and what wasn't.

"And unicorns?" I asked Nico. "Are they real?" I liked this game of not remembering. I liked not being certain of anything. I liked this space between . . . the doubt. It made me feel free. It was like a theta state, that liminal space between waking and dreaming.

This is valuable territory for creative people. When you write, paint, draw, it feels like magic to find this place of soft focus, to not be sure, to allow your imagination full rein. The rational mind is more like a donkey—stubborn and sure.

Frank Ostaseski, Buddhist teacher and author of one of my favorite books, *The Five Invitations*, calls this "don't know mind." In Zen, it's also called "beginner's mind." It describes the mindset you have when you are new to something, free of preconceived notions and expectations and in a place of curiosity.

Being an expert. Having nothing more to learn. Being sure. These are all wonder killers. Let's practice not knowing. Let's practice saying *I wonder . . .* more often. Let's remember that life is just one big experiment. And the more we learn, the less we know. That sometimes, the things we are most certain about turn out to be entirely different.

TRY THIS:

One thing I notice about parenting these days is that as soon as my kids ask a question, say, "Mom, which animal is the fastest in the world?" someone will inevitably reach for their phone: "Oh, let me google that for you!"

I find myself saying to them (insert exaggerated grandfatherly voice), "Back when I was your age, we didn't have Google! We had to pick up an actual book—the encyclopedia that one of those traveling salesmen sold door-to-door!"

My invitation is to linger a few beats longer in the not-knowing. In fact, for the next 24 hours, don't google *anything*. This will be tricky for most of us! It's an automatic impulse, a habit we have ingrained in our muscle memory. You might feel some frustration and withdrawal.

But stay in the not-knowing even if it feels uncomfortable. Wonder a bit. Muse. Realize it's okay to not know. Imagine all the possibilities.

Refuse to know anything for 24 hours.

> IF YOUR MIND IS EMPTY . . .
> IT IS OPEN TO EVERYTHING.
> IN THE BEGINNER'S MIND
> THERE ARE MANY POSSIBILITIES,
> BUT IN THE EXPERT'S MIND
> THERE ARE FEW.
>
> –SHUNRYU SUZUKI, *ZEN MIND, BEGINNER'S MIND*

48. Ask the Dictionary for Advice

DURING MY FINAL YEAR IN COLLEGE, I had the big breakup. You know the one. The one that brings you to your knees, where you can't speak for days, where the anguish is so crushing you don't know if you'll ever recover. It was a love-at-first-sight kind of thing—we spotted each other in a café, and a few espressos later, we were shacked up for the next two years. If there is such a thing as past lives, I'm sure we must have known each other in many.

A few months after the breakup, I met Dan in one of my classes. He was funny and adorable and loved to take photos as much as I did. I agreed to go out with him because he made me laugh and forget my troubles. We played, went on photo safaris, took road trips, and cracked each other up. And then, just as quickly as he came in, he left. He stood me up for a movie, then later explained that his ex-girlfriend had come back into town and that they were going to try again.

I was furious that I had dared to open my heart again. Even just a little bit. I felt duped, both by him and by the Universe, and I was overwhelmed that all of my wounds that had begun to heal were being ripped open again.

I remember flopping on the couch in total exasperation and anger, tears pouring down my face, and asking God, the room, whoever was listening, "WHY DID THAT ASSHOLE HAVE TO COME INTO MY LIFE?" (I think I actually asked this at full volume to the empty house.) And because I sometimes played a game where I asked the dictionary a question and opened randomly to get clarity and guidance, that's what I did in this moment. I grabbed the dictionary and asked again through my blinding tears, "Why did Dan come into my life?"

The word I got was *nepenthe*: "a grief-banishing drug; something that eases sorrow or pain." My breath caught in my throat.

188

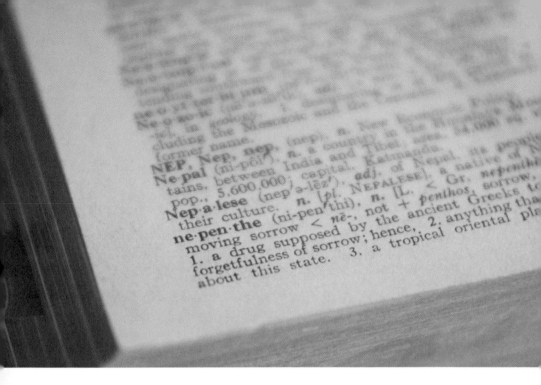

Oh my God, I thought. Dan *was my nepenthe*. He had gifted me six glorious weeks of healing laughter. He had pulled me out of one of the darkest places I had ever gone. He wasn't supposed to stick around. He was supposed to be a simple gift.

Immediately, my heart was awash in forgiveness. All the anger was replaced by gratitude for this boy and to the Universe for bringing him when I needed him most.

But allow me to rewind for a moment so I can tell you about the dictionary. My friends and I discovered this divination-with-the-dictionary thing by accident. We were playing a game of Balderdash, drinking wine, and just generally being silly.

My friend Chris suddenly said, "Oh, dictionary, tell me what the name of my firstborn child will be!" Then he opened the dictionary and pointed randomly to a word.

"Drivel!" he proclaimed.

And we all laughed at how perfect that was.

Another friend grabbed the dictionary. "Okay, dictionary, tell me what I'm supposed to do with my life!"

Again, the answer was fitting. We all got a little bit nervous, but also excited.

My friend Laura, who was the most New Agey of the bunch, took the dictionary in her hands and asked earnestly, "Who is sending us these messages?" The word she pointed to was *magpie*.

We all nodded. *Okay, a chattering magpie, a bird whispering in our ear.* We didn't think much of it.

But that night, Chris told his mom about our strange experience with the dictionary. When he got to the part about magpie, her eyes got wide. "In some Native American folklore, the magpie is the messenger between the two worlds."

So whenever any of us needed guidance in our life, we would get into a meditative state, think about what we needed clarity on, open the dictionary, and point to a word. Apparently, this is called *bibliomancy*, and humans have been doing this for centuries, mostly with sacred texts like the Bible and the Koran.

Want to give it a try? Here are some questions that I find super helpful:
- Give me a word for something I should be aware of that I'm not aware of.
- What's the energy I need to draw on right now?
- What would help with the situation I'm struggling with?
- What would bring me more joy?

Words carry worlds of ideas and meaning. When you choose your word, it might seem abstract at first, but use it as a doorway to clarity and insight. Imagine what medicine the word might hold for you.

49. Remember a Moment of Synchronicity

PEOPLE SAY ALL SORTS OF THINGS ABOUT SERENDIPITY. *There are no coincidences!* or *They are just coincidences!* Some say it is the Universe speaking to them, others claim it is chance, still others, magic. One of my favorite authors, Rachel Naomi Remen (who wrote *Kitchen Table Wisdom*), refers to it as a "glimpse of a deeper order," which I like. Whenever I encounter a serendipitous moment, it gives me a thrill, goose bumps in the very best way, and a feeling that I am part of something greater than myself.

I rely on synchronicity as a guide and as a way to tune in to spirit. I see it as my personal thumbs-up from the Universe, as in: "Thumbs-up, sister! You're on the right track!"

One of my favorite serendipity stories happened more than twenty years ago when I had first moved to San Francisco and was working as a salesperson in a clothing boutique. I was chatting with a customer one day and the singer/songwriter Ben Harper came up in conversation. I found myself gushing.

"I adore Ben Harper!" And then I added, "There are artists you admire and there are artists you want to *meet*. I want to meet Ben Harper."

A few hours later, when I finished my shift, I decided to take a different route home. It was a sunny day, and I thought, *Why rush home? Let's just wander for a while.* I headed in the opposite direction of my house and strolled through Pacific Heights and the Fillmore District.

Just when I started to get tired, I saw a bus coming. *Perfect*, I thought. As I hopped onto the 22 Fillmore, my heart skipped several beats. I practically floated down the aisle, as if carried by some unseen force, and sat down right next to Ben Harper.

Let me repeat.

I sat down right next to Ben Harper.

As my heart leaped even further outside my chest, I tapped him on the shoulder. He pulled the earbuds out of his ears and leaned toward me.

"Is your name Ben?" I asked tentatively.

He nodded.

"Wow . . . ," I whispered, my eyes wide. "Just a few hours ago I said I wanted to meet you. I can't believe how fast the Universe works."

He smiled and we shared a moment of pure wonder. That moment is permanently seared into my mind—an unforgettable instance of awe, connection, and joy.

That wouldn't be the last time I met Ben Harper. Years later, I met him backstage at a concert and was blown away when he told me he remembered me from the bus.

But here's the other thing about the name Ben. Throughout my twenties, I would always say, *I'm going to marry a Ben or have a child named Ben.* It was my favorite name, but also an intuitive knowing. My friends all knew this about me and would try to introduce me to any single men named Ben they met at parties.

But when I fell in love with Matt and decided to get married, I thought, *Well, I'm marrying a Matt, so I guess we're going to be having a Ben.* Again, it wasn't a desire so much as a knowing.

This knowing helped carry me through several painful years of infertility. We would always talk about Ben, and say, "Well, when Ben comes . . .," and "When Ben's here . . ." And it always surprised me that the name was never a discussion. Matt had strong opinions, so I was amazed that he was such an easy yes to Ben's name. And hilariously, it never even occurred to us that we'd have a girl.

Our son Ben did eventually arrive. And when he was a few months old, Matt's parents came to visit us one evening. They said, "Matt, we never told you this, but when we adopted you [they brought him home from the hospital when he was six weeks old], I believe the nurses had named you Ben. We changed your name to Matthew."

Matt and I looked at each other, stunned. Ben was the first name Matt had ever heard. Of course it had resonance for him.

And me, well, it turns out I married a Ben *and* had a Ben.

I can't say for sure what synchronicity means. I do know that these coincidences, these moments of synchronicity, delight and nourish me in the best ways. They are an affirmation of my connectedness to spirit, to my path, and proof that I am aligned with my intuition and heart. They are like gifts from the Universe, reminders that magic exists, and that I am being held by unseen forces.

What about you? What stories of synchronicity do you have? How do you feel when they happen?

Ben!

50. Talk to Someone's Higher Self

ONE DAY, I was talking with my friend SARK about a conflict I was having and she said, "You know you can talk to someone's higher self, don't you?" She went on. "Just call upon *your* higher self in meditation or some kind of quiet moment. Then imagine the other person's higher self. Tell them whatever you need to tell them, express the outcome that you are hoping for, make whatever requests you need to make of them. On some level, they will hear you."

One day I decided to try it.

I was in the throes of a really tender part of my divorce. Grief and anxiety had taken their toll on my nervous system, and it was hard to sleep or find any peace. But as I was walking in my neighborhood, I thought about the guy I'd been flirting with on the soccer field. We had originally met in a yoga class, but then I ran into him during my son's soccer practice and discovered he was a parent too. And single! And handsome! And so we would chat each Tuesday evening on the field as our kids played.

But this day as I walked, I remembered what SARK had said. *I'll give it a try . . .* , I thought. In my mind, I imagined saying to him: *Okay, hot soccer dude. Here's the deal. I'm super attracted to you. And I am in dire need of a healing touch. I've been through the wringer lately, and I think I just need someone to hold me. I don't need you to be my boyfriend. I'm not ready for any kind of relationship. I just need healing touch.*

I laughed at myself and then let it go.

Two hours later, I received a message from him on Facebook. (By this time we had graduated to being Facebook friends but had never messaged each other.)

"So when do I get to see you next?" he wrote.

I gasped. This sounded forward. Unmistakable. Beyond flirty. Had his higher self heard me? Then he invited me to his house for tea the next day. Was I seeing air quotes around the word *tea*? Or did he literally mean tea?

The next day I arrived at a pretty little cottage, and he ushered me into the garden. As I passed through the house, I noticed altars everywhere. The air smelled like sage and palo santo, and there were crystals and other mysterious metaphysical woo all over the house.

We drank tea and chatted for a long time on the deck. And then, quietly, he turned toward me, wrapped his entire six-foot frame around my body, and held me. No words. Just held me. Just like I had told his higher self I wanted.

Then he asked me if he could do a healing over my body. Intuitively, I nodded. He burned things. He blew smoke into my open palms. He flicked holy water over me. He waved owl feathers across my heart. He sang songs in another language. I didn't understand exactly what was happening, but I knew that his higher self had heard me. My prayer for healing touch had been received and he was clearly the right guy for the job.

I said to him, "This might sound strange, but I sent you a telepathic telegram yesterday."

"I know." He nodded. "I got it."

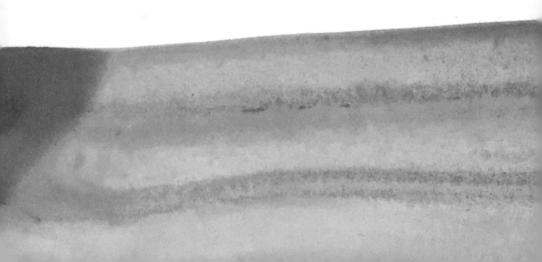

You ready to try?

This is an experiment that might be hard to quantify, but let's give it a try anyway. Is there someone you'd like to send a message to? Who pops into your mind first? That will be the perfect person.

- Maybe it's someone who needs your forgiveness and compassion.
- Maybe it's someone you are in conflict with and this meditation will help soften the barriers.
- Maybe it's someone you deeply love and you want to send them loving energy.
- Maybe it's a doctor you will be visiting soon who you need to listen to you deeply so that you can get the proper care. Talk to their higher self and tell them what you most need.
- Maybe it's your future partner (who you haven't even met yet!) and you can tell them how excited you are to meet them and love them.

Use your imagination and see what happens. It's all just an experiment.

51. Make a Blessing Stick

WHEN I WENT TO MY FRIEND JAN STAMOS'S ART OPENING one weekend, I immediately fell in love with a bundle of colorful sticks she had on display. They looked magical—rich with color and texture—and felt like they had a story.

"Ohhhh, what are these?" I gushed.

"I call them blessing sticks," she told me. "I use scraps of fabric, recycled sari ribbon, yarn, beads, anything that catches my eye, and wrap the sticks while I think about the person I am making it for. If I am making them for a show, I just infuse them with good energy and blessings. Come over to the studio one day and we will make some together!"

Okay, y'all. This is the most relaxing and forgiving art project ever. They are so fun and easy to make! And you can't mess them up—they *always* turn out beautifully! It has become my new go-to gift for anyone I want to love up and an activity that's so much fun to do with other people.

Here's what you'll need:
- Strips of fabric (I ordered recycled sari ribbon online and they are beyond gorgeous). You can also use yarn or other types of ribbon.
- Sticks! You can use driftwood, bamboo, twigs, and sticks you find out in nature, dowels, or big (twelve-inch, non-food-grade) cinnamon sticks.
- Scissors (for cutting the fabric).

How to make a blessing stick:
- This is where you really just follow your intuition and trust the process. Find pieces of fabric and colors that delight you. Cut pieces that are long enough to wrap at least once around the stick or wrap a longer piece several times around the stick. Then tie a little knot to secure it.
- No need to cut off the ends of the ribbon—I love how they create a fun texture when they are sticking out—but you might also want to tuck the ends underneath the ribbon next to it for a cleaner look.
- While you are wrapping the stick with beautiful bits of color, think about the person you are making it for, which might be you! Think about all that you want to bless this person with—*joy, love and partnership, adventures in nature*—and consider all that you appreciate about them. This will infuse the stick with blessings and let the person know how loved they are.

The photos you see on the previous pages are from our day making a blessing stick for my friend Lily! She was starting a brand-new chapter of her life and my friend Mati and I wanted to shower her with some love. I brought driftwood and sari scraps to the park and as we added each ribbon we declared what we were blessing her with. "This one is for love! This one is for trips to Costa Rica! This one is for unexpected magic!"

In addition to wrapping sticks, I have wrapped mason jars and filled them with things I appreciate about that person written on tiny scraps of paper. I have wrapped twigs with embroidery floss. You can wrap almost anything! Just trust your intuition and know that you are giving something from your heart. The best kind of gift!

52. Sprinkle Your Sparkle

THERE IS A POSTAL WORKER I USED TO SEE EVERY FEW DAYS, back when I had a jewelry business and mailed packages regularly. I had the impression that she was a bit crabby or just didn't like me, but suddenly at the window one day everything changed. I was pregnant with my first son, and she asked me about the baby, when he was due, what his name was, etc. When I told her Ben, she exclaimed, "That's a terrible name!" and I laughed as she scrunched up her face in mock disgust.

Then she surprised me by saying she wouldn't sell me a whole sheet of stamps (only ten) because, "This way you'll come back to the window sooner."

We all want to be connected.

As I walked away, I remembered Margarita from my old post office, who I would see nearly every day, the one who got mad at me when I started using the automated postal machine for my priority packages. Who said, "Girl, if I ever see you using that machine again and not waiting in line to see me, you're gonna get it!"

Either I have a special way with the ladies at the post office, or we are all hungry for human connection.

We forget that our presence matters. **Everywhere we go, we matter.** We think, *Oh, I won't go to that meeting, that party, that class. No one will miss me anyway.*

But the truth is, we all matter and we are all missed.

At one of his concerts, the singer/songwriter Michael Franti talked about how when any of us walk into a room—the grocery store, the hair salon, wherever—we have an impact. How we show up is both a choice and an opportunity. He calls it sprinkling our sparkle! And reminds himself that his energy has an impact on those around him, and he can choose to use it for the positive.

We should all want to be responsible for the energy we bring to a space, for the impact we have on the world outside of ourselves.

When I was online dating, I used to set an intention before every single date. Before I would get out of the car to go into the restaurant or café, I would close my eyes, put my hand on my heart, and say, "May this date be delightful in some way, whether or not it's a yes to a second date. May it flow with ease and joy." This was partly me setting an intention, but it was also priming me to look for what was delightful about this person, even if we never went out again. It was managing my own fears and cynicism about dating, and consciously choosing to bring my sparkle.

And guess what? Being someone who looks for the good in others is incredibly attractive! Who doesn't want to spend time with someone who is looking for something to delight in?

Give it a try this week. Set an intention before you walk into a meeting, a date, or a class. Just put your hand on your heart and say, "May I show up with compassion . . . ," or "May I bring my most authentic self to this conversation . . . ," or "May I delight in this experience even though I'm a bit nervous. . . ." Whatever feels true for you. See if you notice a shift in your energy and in the energy of others as a result of this simple declaration. Let's sprinkle our sparkle as much as we can.

Joy is a practice.

It's a muscle. It gets stronger when we use it, when we tend to it with our attention. We're going to be like gardeners of joy. And for no good reason, except that life is messy and full of hard things, and that's exactly why we strengthen this muscle. So that we can reach for it when we need it most. So that when we respond to life, we are heartier and more resilient.

Poet Ross Gay says it beautifully: "Joy and delight are rigorous. More rigorous than misery."

Joy is indeed more rigorous than we might think! It is as rigorous as staying present. If you've ever tried to meditate, you know how much muscle it actually involves. To just sit and watch your thoughts. To notice how they run amok. To see the stories and the judgments and to-do lists float by like ticker tape. It takes effort to bring ourselves back to what is actually here, what is true, what we can touch.

In the same way, it takes practice to bring ourselves closer to wonder or delight or gratitude. It requires a softening of the heart. An openness and a willingness to see what else is possible. It's not a clenched fist, but an open hand.

My wish is that as a result of growing your sense of wonder and curiosity, you will also grow your joy. That you will learn how to tend it. That you understand how our joy lives in relationship to our grief and our tender spots. That our joy is not separate from or outside of the messiness of our lives. That there is no need to be somewhere better than where you are right now.

I used to babysit an adorable seven-year-old named Chloe when I was in college in Santa Barbara. I remember one day she asked if we could ride the city bus. "Sure!" I exclaimed. "Where should we go?"

"Oh, no," she replied. "I don't want to *go* anywhere," she explained. "I just want to ride the bus!"

And so, we rode the bus through town, not going anywhere at all, not even getting off the bus until we completed the route and ended up where we started. We held hands, watched the world go by out the window, and delighted in the people we chatted with during the ride.

My wish for you is a similar kind of delight in the journey, of nowhere in particular to go, but awake to all the magic right under our noses. Let's put on our wonder goggles. Let's build our joy muscles. Let's share what we love.

Thank you!

ACKNOWLEDGMENTS

THANK YOU TO Ben and Nico for showing me the wonder that is loving you! And for being so enthusiastic and inquisitive at every phase of this project. You added to the joy of creating it with your curiosity.

Thank you to my parents, Joan and Bob, for nurturing the creative creature in me, and to my beautiful, talented sister Caroline for always having my back. Also, big love to the rest of the Loewengart family—Matthew, Caleb, and Ruby.

Thank you to Lilly Ghahremani for seeing the shimmer in this project right from the start.

Thank you to Rachel Cole for your coaching wizardry and to Emma Brownson for your design genius.

Deepest gratitude to my soul family, Christina Sanders, Mati Rose McDonough, Brigette Scheel, Sasha Wizansky, Kelly Rae Roberts, Laurie Wagner, Matt Passmore, SARK, Brené Brown, Jesse Bloom, Marcia Gagliardi, Laurel Bleadon-Maffei, Myriam Joseph, Micki and Nadie, Bob Reid and Judi Jaeger, Monica Pasqual, Maya Stein, John Nieto, Juna Mustad, Annie Wright, Sherry Richert Belul, Lara Hutner, Keri Smith, Jeff Pitcher, Eric and Stacy Davison, Kate Swoboda, Viola Toniolo, Jen Villeneuve, Chris Harrington, and Jacques Pryor. Your love is the greatest gift!

Thank you to my Friday magic circle and to the Lovebombers.

Soyolmaa Lkhagvadorj, you brought this book to life with your curiosity and your smarts. Thank you for being my cheerleader!

Thank you to Marta Schooler and the Harper Design team for believing in this project! And so much gratitude to you, Stephanie Stislow, for your gorgeous design. The book became so vibrant and alive in your hands!

And big, wiggly thank-yous to the wonder dogs that bring me daily joy: Jiggly Puff, Izzie, Roxi, Lulu, Shouka, Rupee, Mishra, and Oso.

ATTENTION IS THE
DOORWAY TO
gratitude,
THE DOORWAY
TO WONDER,
THE DOORWAY
TO RECIPROCITY.

–ROBIN WALL KIMMERER

ABOUT THE AUTHOR

Andrea Scher **is an artist, blogger, podcaster, photographer, and online workshop teacher whose work is driven by her belief in the transformative power of creativity.**

She guides women to feel more brave, joyful, and connected through her innovative use of creativity as a springboard for self-empowerment. For nearly two decades, her popular approach has thrilled attendees and listeners, resulting in her award-winning blog *Superhero Journal* and best-selling e-courses. She interviews authors, artists, and other creative thinkers of our time on her *Creative Superheroes* podcast and has been featured in books by Brené Brown and SARK, and in *Lapham's Quarterly* and more.

You can learn more about Andrea at the following social media channels:
www.andreascher.com
Instagram: @andreascher
Podcast: www.andreascher.com/podcast